CROCHET
TECHNIQUES

CROCHET
TECHNIQUES

Renate Kirkpatrick

SALLYMILNER
PUBLISHING

First published in 2007 by
Sally Milner Publishing Pty Ltd
734 Woodville Road
Binda NSW 2583
AUSTRALIA

© Renate Kirkpatrick 2007

Design:Anna Warren, Warren Ventures Pty Ltd
Editing: Anne Savage
Photography: Tim Connolly
Illustrations: Wendy Gorton, Anna Warren and the author

Printed in China

National Library of Australia Cataloguing-in-Publication data:
Kirkpatrick, Renate, 1951- .
        Crochet techniques.

        ISBN 9781863513715 (pbk.).

        1. Crocheting - Patterns. I. Title.
        (Series : Milner craft series).

        746.434041

Disclaimer
Information and instructions given in this book are presented in good faith, but no warranty is given nor results guaranteed, nor is freedom from any patent to be inferred. As we have no control over physical conditions surrounding application of information herein contained in this book, the author and publisher disclaim any liability for untoward results.

10 9 8 7 6 5 4 3 2 1

DEDICATION

Dedicated to my grandmother, Carolina, whose exquisite needlework will always be treasured … I wish I had known her … and to all those wonderfully gifted women who throughout the ages worked tirelessly with needles and hooks to improve their homes for the love of their families for neither recognition or gain

ACKNOWLEDGEMENTS

Heartfelt thanks must go to all my students, past and present, who unwittingly proofread my patterns and in doing so dotted all the i's and crossed all the t's—what a wealth of knowledge we've gained over the years.

Thank you to my niece, Tamran, for editing and fine-tuning—your eagle eye never ceases to amaze me.

Thank you, Libby Renney, for plucking me from the outer reaches of the cosmos—and to the entire staff at Sally Milner publications for affording me this wonderful opportunity.

CONTENTS

WHY SAMPLER RUGS?

Years of teaching have taught me that we all need achievable goals to keep us interested. These sampler rugs grew out of this premise and have become effective teaching tools. The patterns are a mixed bag of stitches to help you gain solid, well-grounded knowledge in crochet. While some of the stitches are a breeze to work, others will require a little more concentration—but there's no equal to the feeling of accomplishment you'll have in the end.

As you make your way through each technique you'll discover a whole range of interesting and useful stitches that you'll want to use over and over again; your confidence will soar and, before you know it, you'll have beautiful heirlooms that will be proudly passed down the generations. Once you've familiarised yourself with the following crochet fundamentals you're ready, set and on your way—enjoy.

BITS AND PIECES YOU'LL NEED

- Collection of crochet hooks in various sizes—standard, Tunisian, double-ended

- Enough yarn of choice to complete your project

- Collection of odd yards for swatches

- Blunt darning needle for sewing in tail-ends

- Scissors

- Rust-proof pins

- Safety pins, markers, short lengths of yarn (for markers)

- Tape measure

- Steel ruler, used as a guide when reading patterns (especially helpful in Jacquard)

CROCHET STITCHES AND TECHNIQUES

READING PATTERNS

Sometimes crochet patterns can be rather wordy, particularly circular motifs that require instruction for each round—this can be a daunting experience, especially for the beginner. My advice is to glance through the pattern and see if there's anything unusual that you need to know, then go back to the beginning and follow the pattern from one comma to the next comma. Everything between those commas is one instruction. For example: 1 ch, dc (US sc) in next 3 sts, means 'make the 1 ch, then work a dc (US sc) in each of the next 3 stitches', and so on. Don't be frightened by the terminology and symbols; you'll soon be familiar with what, to the newcomer, looks like another language. Above all, take your time. If you come across a particularly complicated section and you're having trouble nutting it out, put your work aside for the minute, make yourself a cuppa and take a deep breath. Then, have another go—you'll often find it's not nearly as complicated as you first thought.

And I strongly suggest making use of both the written patterns and diagrams. You will be surprised how much clearer the instructions become.

YARN

My advice is to always to use yarn you like working with (but preferably the same ply as the pattern recommends). I'm not a purist and never shy away from using economy yarns if a colour and/or texture is right for a particular project. Later, when you've gained experience and grown in confidence you may decide to spend a little more on your yarn. Remember to purchase enough of the dye lot to complete your project. It's always better to have a little too much than to run out with two motifs to go. It's also a good idea to keep yarn labels as a reference—if you do run out of yarn before you've finished a project, and that dye lot has run out wherever you purchased it, you can if need be contact the manufacturer.

MULTIPLES

The multiples given for the Classic 36-stitch sampler rug are helpful for determining the foundation chain in other projects, and are explained further in that chapter.

MARKERS

In the past I considered markers a needless interruption to the job at hand and rarely used them. Then one day a particularly complicated project came along, where markers were essential, and I suddenly realised how helpful they really are. The small amount of time it takes to place them saves hours in the long run and I have used them ever since. I use markers to indicate right side or top/bottom of work, first stitch of round, centre stitches in corners—and my crocheting life has never been easier. Commercial markers can be purchased from any craft supplier but safety pins or short yarn off-cuts (which I use) do the job just as well.

SWATCHES

Being usually in too much of a hurry getting on with the project in hand, I've never been a great advocate of making swatches (unless it's a garment where size is an issue). However, I strongly advise making swatches for the Tunisian and crochenit samplers, at least in the beginning while you're working out the technique. Sixteen stitches are usually sufficient to develop the pattern, and doing this is certainly less disheartening than having to pull out 30 after finding the mistake at the beginning of the row.

TENSION

I've deliberately omitted any rug dimensions; how loose or tight you crochet and the few centimetres difference that may result overall aren't vital for these projects. The hook size and yarns given for each project are recommendations only and by no means have to be complied with. It's far more important that your work is consistent, something that is much easier to achieve if you're working within your own comfort zone. These are your projects; work in the hook sizes, colours and yarns you prefer. Enjoyment, knowledge and confidence are the aim—not trying to reproduce the exact same rug, either in size or colour, as mine. A helpful tip for keeping yarn flowing freely is taking it from the centre of the ball. This way the yarn comes to you, not the other way round.

DETERMINING SQUARE SIZE

From time to time fold your square corner to corner to determine how many rows you require before the top corners meet. When coming to the end of the square, try ending with the row most similar to the first row. For example, if the first row was worked in dc (US sc) then finish on a row of dc (US sc) also.

EDGING

When edging your squares/motifs it is imperative that you work the correct number of stitches as stated in the pattern (three stitches in corners and a certain number of stitches between). The top and bottom edges are usually straightforward because the first and last row stitches are clearly visible. It's the two side edges that sometimes pose a bit of a problem because there are no obvious stitches to work. Nevertheless, it's important that the same number of stitches is worked along these sides, even though you may feel that stitches are being squeezed in or too far apart—just work as neatly and evenly as you can. The reason will become clear later, when you are joining the squares/motifs stitch for stitch.

TIPS FOR AN ATTRACTIVE FINISH

It would be a real shame after spending many diligent hours working out the patterns for the squares and motifs only to have your project spoiled by an unsightly overall finish.

In my experience the most common mistakes made in crochet are at the beginning and end of a row due to confusion as to where to work the first and last stitch. If your work has uneven edges that zigzag here and there, or it leans off to the right or left, there's a good chance this fundamental is being overlooked. The following is a guide that I hope will help remedy this frustrating dilemma.

The foundation chain is the number of chains required for the length and/or pattern *plus* the extra chains that are required to accommodate the height of stitch in the row about to be worked.

For example: if trebles (US double crochet) are being used you will need 2 extra chains for the foundation chain and 3 extra chains on each working row. These 3 extra chains are called the *turning chain* and (unless the pattern states otherwise) must always be counted as the *first stitch* of the row or round. This means that in subsequent rows or rounds the turning chain must be treated as a stitch at the end of each previous row or round.

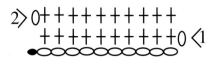

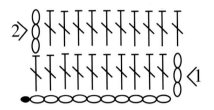

fig 3a stitch placement

fig 3b stitch placement

Stitch in use/abbr. (US term/abbr.)	Turning ch	Work 1st stitch on foundation ch
double crochet/dc (US single crochet/sc)	1 ch	2nd ch from hook
half treble/htr (US half double crochet/hdc)	2 ch	3rd ch from hook
treble/tr (US double crochet/dc)	3 ch	4th ch from hook
double treble/dtr (US treble/tr)	4 ch	5th ch from hook
triple treble/trtr (US double treble/dtr)	5 ch	6th ch from hook
quadruple treble/qtr (US triple treble/trtr)	6 ch	7th ch from hook

WHERE TO WORK THE FIRST STITCH?

For double crochet/dc (US single crochet/sc), insert hook in *first* stitch to start new row:

For all tall posted stitches, insert hook in *second* stitch to start new row. This example shows trebles/tr (US double crochet/dc):

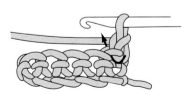

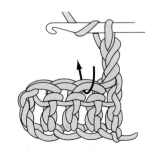

TAIL ENDS

Another common problem arises from the false economy of leaving short tail ends. Leave reasonable length tail ends that can be easily and securely woven in later with a blunt darning needle—nothing spoils your work more than fluffy ends popping up throughout your work. Better still, wherever possible crochet over the ends as you work. And, when joining new yarn try to avoid using knots. They produce weak spots and have the annoying habit of moving to the front of the work.

The following two methods are recommended as the neatest ways of bringing in new yarn, and apply whether changing colour or just bringing in new yarn as the current ball runs out:

◉ working with one colour: place the new yarn along the top of your work and crochet a few stitches over it before the old yarn has run out; then pick up the new and crochet over the old.

◉ working with 2 colours: when 2 loops of last colour remain on hook, drop old colour, pick up new colour and draw through 2 loops.

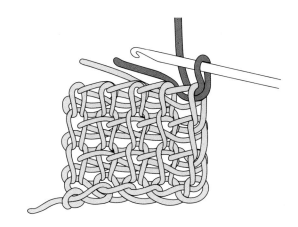

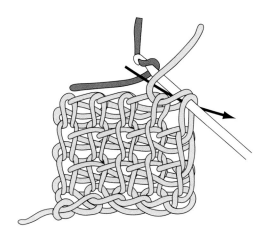

Although both methods are best done at the beginning or end of a row or round, they work equally well wherever you find yourself running out of yarn or needing to change colour.

BLOCKING

With the exception of Tunisian crochet (explained in the instructions for the Tunisian crochet sampler), as a general rule I do not block sampler squares/motifs unless I feel it's absolutely necessary.

As your pile of squares/motifs begins to grow, many of you may become concerned by their slight variations in size and feel the need to block them to the same size. This variation is due to the variety of stitch patterns used in each sampler, and blocking is certainly one way of bringing them into line. However, and I can't stress this enough (you have to trust me here), if the correct number of stitches has been worked around the edge, this will not be a problem and blocking becomes an unnecessary exercise. Later you will be joining the squares stitch for stitch, which naturally brings them together. I also advise draping the finished rug over the back of a lounge for a week or so and letting it drop into shape. If by chance you find a square/motif exceedingly out of line with the rest, it may be worth making it again, using a smaller or larger hook depending on what's required.

When you do want to block:

- place square on a terry towel over a flat surface and, using rust-proof pins, secure each square to shape, lightly steam and allow to dry completely.

- or (I prefer this method for retaining textured stitches) secure squares as above, then liberally apply spray starch and allow to dry completely.

JOINING SQUARES AND MOTIFS

Follow the directions given with the sampler using one of the following joining techniques.

For an invisible join, use mattress stitch (also known as ladder st):

- with right side facing, lay squares or motifs to be joined side by side on a flat surface

- with a blunt-ended darning needle join in back loop of one square/motif

- slide the needle through two loops of second square/motif then two loops of the first again

- repeat a couple of times and draw together firmly

- manually ease the stitches back gently with your fingers

- continue until the join is complete, then

- weave in ends

For a visible or flat join, you have the choice of three methods:

1. **Whip stitch join**: with the wrong sides of square/motif facing and using a blunt-ended darning needle, overcast stitch each corresponding st together to end. Weave in ends.

2. **Slip stitch join**: join with ss in first sts and ss each corresponding st together to end. Weave in ends.

3. **dc (US sc) join**: join with dc (US sc) in first st, dc (US sc) each corresponding st together to end. Weave in ends. When joining with dc (US sc), start with slip knot on hook, insert hook into st or sp indicated and draw up a loop, YO and draw through both loops on hook (counts as first dc [US sc]).

THE BASICS
SLIP KNOT

When making your foundation chain, start with a slip knot rather than just tying an ordinary knot. It is neater and allows the next chain (chain 1) to flow rather than being tugged through the loop just made. Never count the loop (on the hook) as a chain or stitch.

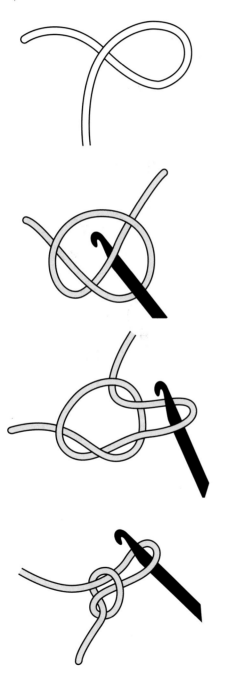

FOUNDATION CHAIN/CH

This term refers to the number of chains required for a particular length and/or pattern plus the extra chains required to accommodate the stitch height:

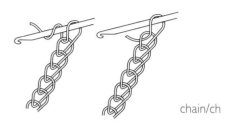

chain/ch

SLIP STITCH/SS

Insert hook into st, YO and draw yarn through st and loop on hook:

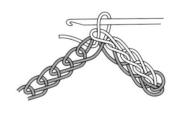

DOUBLE CROCHET/DC
(US single crochet/sc)

Working along foundation ch, insert hook into 2nd ch from hook, YO and draw loop through st (2 loops on hook), YO and draw yarn through both loops (dc [US sc] made):

HALF TREBLE/HTR
(US half double crochet/hdc)

Working along foundation ch, YO, insert hook into 3rd ch from hook, YO and draw loop through st (3 loops on hook), YO and draw yarn through all 3 loops (htr [US hdc] made):

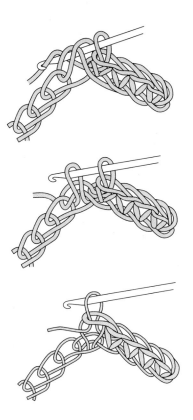

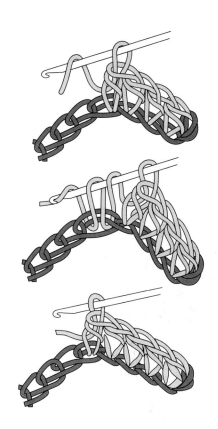

TREBLE/TR
(US double crochet/dc)

Working along foundation ch, YO, insert hook into 4th ch from hook, YO and draw yarn through st (3 loops on hook), YO, draw through 2 loops, YO and draw through last 2 loops (tr [US dc] made):

DOUBLE TREBLE/DTR
(US treble crochet/tr)

YO twice, insert hook in st or sp and pull up a loop, YO and draw through 2 loops on hook 3 times:

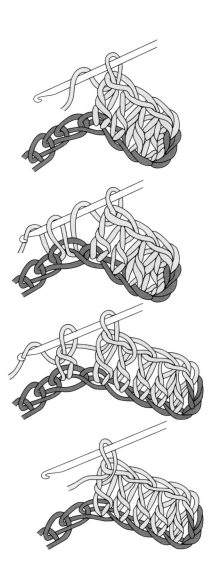

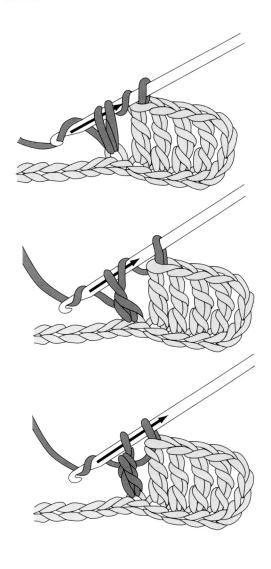

FRONT OR BACK LOOP ONLY

Work only in loop indicated by arrow:

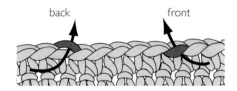

POST STITCH (FP OR BP)

Work around post of stitch indicated in row or rows below, inserting hook in direction of arrow:

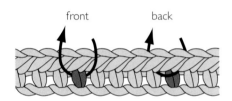

FINISHING OFF (CASTING-OFF STITCH)

With the last stitch complete, cut yarn and draw through the loop on hook, pull tight to close the loop. Weave in end. With slippery yarn, draw through the loop twice (make an extra chain) and pull down very tightly with your thumb to close. Weave in end.

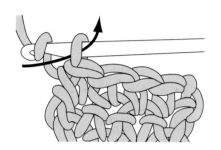

THE PROJECTS

CLASSIC 36-STITCH SAMPLER
AVERAGE TO ADVANCED LEVEL

This beautiful traditional afghan incorporates 36 interesting and useful stitches that you will want to use over and over again.

— SEE PG 50 —

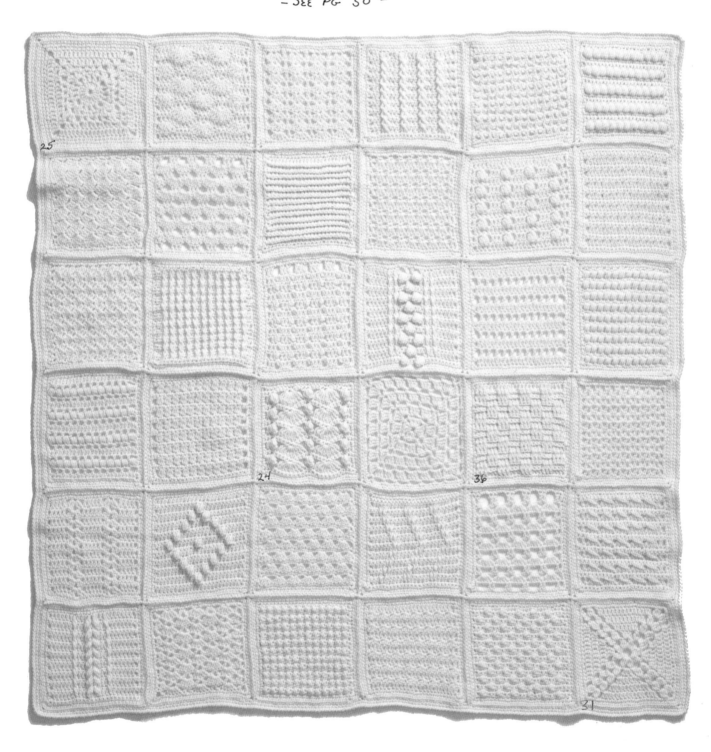

REQUIREMENTS For the rug in the photo I used a 5.00 (US H) crochet hook and approximately 25 × 50 g balls of Cream Panda Carnival 8-ply Pure Wool.

EDGING FOR INDIVIDUAL CLASSIC SAMPLER SQUARES

I recommend that as you complete each square according to the instructions you then finish it with these two rounds of edging. If you don't edge as you go you will end up with a pile of 36 squares needing to be done one after the other—very tedious.

Round 1: right side facing, 1 ch, work 3 dc (US sc) in same corner, work 25 dc (US sc) evenly spaced to next corner, 3 dc (US sc) in corner, repeat around square, join with ss in first dc (US sc) — 112 dc (US sc).

Round 2: ch 1, dc (US sc) in same st and in each st across to next corner st, 3 dc (US sc) in corner st, repeat around, join with ss in first dc (US sc) — 120 dc (US sc).

MARKERS

Where (*right side*) is indicated, loop a short piece of yarn around any stitch on the side facing *before* work is turned. Also use markers to easily identify corner stitches in edging

MULTIPLES

Multiples plus numbers are given wherever they are appropriate, and can come in handy for other projects.

For example: multiples of 4 + 2 ch—the beginning chain would require 10 ch, 14 ch, 18 ch, 22 ch, etc., or any number divisible by 4 plus an additional 2 chains.

ABBREVIATIONS

ch	chain
ss	slip stitch
dc (US sc)	double crochet (US single crochet)
tr (US dc)	treble (US double crochet)
htr (US hdc)	half treble (US half double crochet)
dtr (US tr)	double treble (US treble)
trtr (US dtr)	triple treble (US double treble)
qtr (US trtr)	quadruple treble (US triple treble)
BPtr (US BPdc)	Back Post treble (US Back Post double crochet)
FPtr (US FPdc)	Front Post treble (US Front Post double crochet)
FPhtr (US FPhdc)	Front Post half treble (US Front Post half double crochet)
YO	yarn over
sp	space
st	stitch

CLASSIC SAMPLER DIAGRAM SYMBOLS

◯ = chain ch

● = slip stitch ss/sl st

+ = double crochet (US single crochet) dc (US sc)

T = half treble (US half double crochet) htr (US hdc)

† = treble (US double crochet) tr (US dc)

‡ = double treble (US treble) dtr (US tr)

= triple treble (US double treble) trtr (US dtr)

= quadruple treble (US triple treble) qtr (US trtr)

a   b   c   = work in back loops

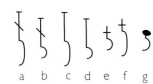

a   b   c   = work in front loops

a   b   c   d   e   f   g   = back post BPtr (US BPdc) BPhtr (US BPhdc) BPdc (US BPsc) BPss

a   b   c   d   e   f   g   = front post FPtr (US FPdc) FPhtr (US FPhdc) FPdc (US FPsc) FPss

a   b   c   = decrease

◀ = finish off

◁ = bring in new yarn/colour

⌒ = unused ch

⟨   ⟩ = row turn

a   b   = puff stitch

a   b   c   d   = beginning clusters

a   b   c   d   e   f   = clusters foundation one stitch cluster (FOSC)

= one stitch cluster (OSC)

= beginning popcorns

a   b   c   = popcorns

= wrap or offset stitch

= bullions with number of wraps

a   b   c   = long or spike stitch

⊠ = reverse dc (US sc) (crab st)

⊠ = reverse dc (US sc) (crab st) in front loop

STITCH GUIDE

Front Post treble/FPtr (US Front Post double crochet/FPdc)

YO, insert hook from front to back around post of next stitch, YO and pull up a loop even with last st worked and complete as a tr (US dc).

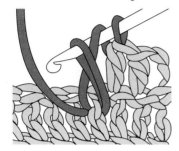

Back Post treble/BPtr (US Back Post double crochet/BPdc)

YO, insert hook from back to front around post of next stitch, YO and pull up a loop even with last stitch worked and complete as treble (US dc).

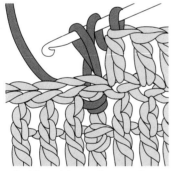

Front Post half treble/FPhtr (US Front Post half double crochet/FPdc)

YO, insert hook from front to back around post of next st, YO and pull up a loop, YO and draw through all 3 loops on hook.

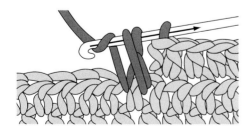

Beginning cluster 3 ch, (YO, insert hook in ring and pull up a loop, YO and draw through 2 loops on hook) twice, YO and draw through all 3 loops on hook.

Cluster YO, insert hook in stitch or space and pull up a loop, YO and draw through 2 loops on hook) 3 times, YO and draw through all 4 loops on hook.

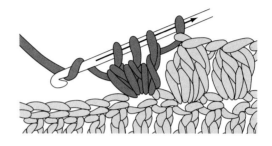

Popcorn Work 5 tr (US dc) or htr (US hdc) in st or sp, drop loop from hook, insert hook in first st of group, hook dropped loop and draw through, 1 ch to close.

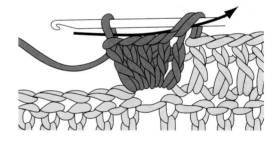

Puff stitch (YO, insert hook in st or space, YO and pull up a loop even with hook) 3 or 4 times, YO and draw through all 7 or 9 loops on hook, 1 ch to close.

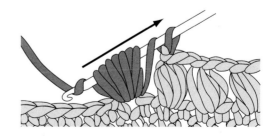

SQUARE 1:
ALIGNED PUFF STITCH

Multiples of 2 ch.

This pattern uses a 9-loop puff stitch and 1 ch to close.

Begin with 26 ch.

Row 1: dc (US sc) in second ch from hook, *1 ch, skip next ch, dc (US sc) in next ch, repeat from * across — 25 sts.

Row 2: (right side) 2 ch, turn, *(work puff st in next 1ch sp, 1 ch to close), 1 ch, repeat from * across, htr (US hdc) in last dc (US sc) — 12 puffs.

Row 3: 1 ch, turn, dc (US sc) in first htr (US hdc), 1 ch, *dc (US sc) in next 1ch sp (between puffs), 1 ch, repeat from * across, dc (US sc) in top of beginning ch — 25 sts.

Repeat Rows 2 and 3 to desired size.
Do not finish off. See notes on edging.

SQUARE 2:
ALTERNATE PUFF STITCH

Multiples of 4 + 2 ch.

The puff stitch used in this pattern is a 7-loop st with no closing ch.

Begin with 26 ch.

Row 1: (right side) dc (US sc) in second ch from hook and in each ch — 25 dc (US sc).

Row 2: 1 ch, turn, dc (US sc) in first 4 dc (US sc), *puff st, dc (US sc) in next 3 dc (US sc), repeat from * to last dc (US sc), dc (US sc) in last dc (US sc) — 5 puff sts.

Row 3: 1 ch, turn, dc (US sc) in each st across.

Row 4: 1 ch, turn, dc (US sc) in first 2 dc (US sc), puff st in next dc (US sc), *dc (US sc) in next 3 dc (US sc), puff st in next dc (US sc), repeat from * across to last 2 dc (US sc), dc (US sc) in last 2 dc (US sc) — 6 puff sts.

Row 5: 1 ch, turn, dc (US sc) in each st across.

Repeat Rows 2 to 5 to desired size.
Do not finish off. See notes on edging.

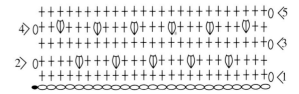

SQUARE 3:
ALTERNATE MESH STITCH
Multiples of 2 +1 ch.

Begin with 27 ch.

Row 1: (right side) tr (US dc) in 4th ch from hook and in each ch across — 25 sts

Row 2: 4 ch (counts as first tr [US dc] plus 1 ch), turn, skip next tr (US dc), *tr (US dc) in next tr (US dc), 1 ch, skip next tr (US dc), repeat from * across, tr (US dc) in top of beginning ch — 12 x 1ch spaces.

Row 3: 3 ch, turn, tr (US dc) in each 1ch space and in each tr (US dc) across — 25 tr (US dc).

Repeat Rows 2 and 3 to desired size.

Do not finish off. See notes on edging.

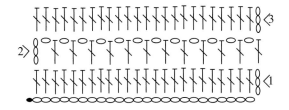

SQUARE 4:
DOUBLES
Multiples of 2 ch.

Begin with 26 ch.

Row 1: dc (US sc) in second ch from hook and in each ch across — 25 dc (US sc).

Row 2: (right side) 3 ch (counts as first tr [US dc]), turn, skip next dc (US sc), *2 tr (US dc) in next dc (US sc), skip next dc (US sc), repeat from * across to last dc (US sc), tr (US dc) in last dc (US sc) — 24 tr (US dc).

Row 3: 1 ch, turn, 2 dc (US sc) in first tr (US dc), dc (US sc) in each tr (US dc) across — 25 dc (US sc).

Repeat Rows 2 and 3 to desired size.
    Do not finish off. See notes on edging.

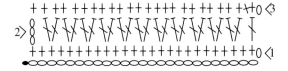

SQUARE 5: COBBLE STITCH

Multiples of 2 ch.

Double treble/dtr (US tr) is used in this pattern.

Begin with 26 ch.

Row 1: (right side) dc (US sc) in 2nd ch from hook and in each ch across — 25 dc (US sc).

Row 2: 1 ch, turn, *dc (US sc) in first dc (US sc), dtr (US tr) in next dc (US sc), repeat from * across to last dc (US sc), dc (US sc) in last dc (US sc) — 25 sts.

Row 3: 1 ch, turn, dc (US sc) in each st across — 25 dc (US sc).

Repeat Rows 2 and 3 to desired size.
    Do not finish off. See notes on edging.

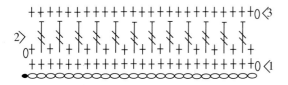

SQUARE 6: HORIZONTAL RIB

No multiple required for this pattern.

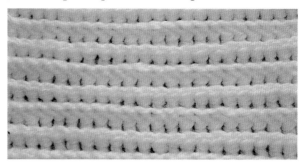

Begin with 27 ch, loosely worked.

Row 1: (right side) tr (US dc) in 4th ch from hook and in each ch across — 25 sts.

Row 2: 2 ch, turn, work FPtr (US FPdc) around the post of next tr (US dc) and in each st across — 25 sts.

Row 3: 2 ch, turn, work BPtr (US BPdc) around the post of each st across — 25 sts.

Repeat Rows 2 and 3 to desired size.
    Do not finish off. See notes on edging.

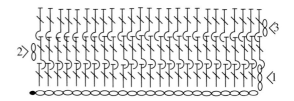

SQUARE 7: PARALLEL RIB

Multiples of 2 + 1 ch.

Begin with 27 ch.

Row 1 (right side) htr (US hdc) in 3rd ch from hook and in each ch across — 25 htr (US hdc).

Row 2: 2 ch, turn, htr (US hdc) in next htr (US hdc) and in each htr (US hdc) across — 25 htr (US hdc).

Row 3: 2 ch, turn, htr (US hdc) in next htr (US hdc), *work FPhtr (US FPhdc) around post of htr (US hdc) below next htr (US hdc), (skip htr [US hdc] behind FPhtr [US FPhdc]), htr (US hdc) in next htr (US hdc), repeat from *across, htr (US hdc) in turning ch — 25 sts.

Row 4: 2 ch, turn, htr (US hdc) in next htr (US hdc) and in each st across — 25 htr (US hdc).

Row 5: 2 ch, turn, htr (US hdc) in next htr (US hdc), *work FPhtr (US FPhdc) around post of next FPhtr (US FPhdc) below, (skip htr [US hdc] behind FPhtr [US FPhdc]), htr (US hdc) in next htr (US hdc), repeat from * across, htr (US hdc) in turning ch — 25 sts.

Repeat Rows 4 and 5 to 12 mm (½ in) from desired size, finishing with row 4.

Last Row: 2 ch, turn, htr (US hdc) in each st to end — 25 htr (US hdc).

Do not finish off. See notes on edging.

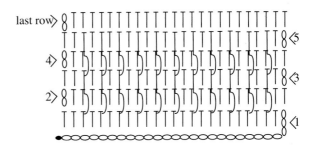

SQUARE 8: CHEVRON RIB

Multiples of 7 + 4 ch.

Notes for Front Post treble/FPtr (US Front Post double crochet/FPdc):

1. Always skip dc (US sc) behind each FP st throughout pattern.

2. FP sts are worked on row below dc (US sc) row.

Begin with 26 ch.

Row 1: dc (US sc) in second ch from hook and in each ch across — 25 dc (US sc).

Row 2: (right side) 2 ch, turn, htr (US hdc) in next dc (US sc) and each dc (US sc) across — 25 htr (US hdc)

Row 3 and all wrong-side rows: 1 ch, turn, dc (US sc) in each st across and in top of beginning ch — 25 dc (US sc).

Row 4: 2 ch, turn, htr (US hdc) in next 2 dc (US sc), *(work FPtr [US FPdc] around post of st below next dc [US sc]) twice, htr (US hdc) in next 5 dc (US sc), repeat from *across to last dc (US sc), htr (US hdc) in last dc (US sc) — 19 htr (US hdc), 6 FPtr (US FPdc).

Row 6: 2 ch, turn, htr (US hdc) in next 3 dc (US sc), *(work FPtr [US FPdc] around post of st below next dc [US sc]) twice, htr (US hdc) in next 5 dc (US sc), repeat from * across — 19 htr (US hdc), 6 FPtr (US FPdc).

Row 8: 2 ch, turn, htr (US hdc) in next 4 dc (US sc), *(work FPtr [US FPdc] around post of st below next dc [US sc]) twice, htr (US hdc) in next 5 dc (US sc), repeat from * across to last 4 dc (US sc), htr (US hdc) in last 4 dc (US sc) — 19 htr (US hdc), 6 FPtr (US FPdc).

Row 10: 2 ch, turn, htr (US hdc) in next 5 dc (US sc), *(work FPtr [US FPdc] around post of st below next dc [US sc]) twice, htr (US hdc) in next 5 dc (US sc), repeat from * across to last 3 dc (US sc), htr (US hdc) in last 3 dc (US sc) — 19 htr (US hdc), 6 FPtr (US FPdc).

Row 12: 2 ch, turn, htr (US hdc) in next 6 dc (US sc), *(work FPtr [US FPdc] around post of st below next dc [US sc]) twice, htr (US hdc) in next 5 dc (US sc), repeat from * across to last 2 dc (US sc), htr (US hdc) in last 2 dc (US sc) — 19 htr (US hdc), 6 FPtr (US FPdc).

Row 14: repeat Row 10.

Row 16: repeat Row 8.

Row 18: repeat Row 6.

Row 20: repeat Row 4.

Row 21: finish on Row 3 — 25 dc (US sc).
    Do not finish off. See notes on edging.

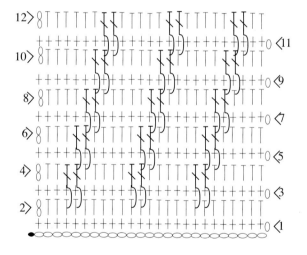

SQUARE 9:
V-STITCH

Multiples of 3 + 1 ch.

V-STITCH

(tr [US dc], 1 ch, tr [US dc]) in same st or sp—V-stitch made.

Begin with 28 ch.

Row 1: V-st in 5th ch from hook, *skip next 2 ch, V-st in next ch, repeat from * across to last 2 ch, tr (US dc) in last ch — 8 V-sts.

Row 2: (right side) 3 ch, turn, V-st in each 1ch sp across, tr (US dc) in top of beginning ch.

Repeat Row 2 to desired size.

Do not finish off. See notes on edging.

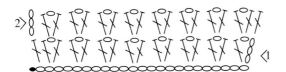

SQUARE 10:
V-STITCH AND SHELL

Multiples of 8 + 5 ch.

V-STITCH

(tr [US dc], 1 ch, tr [US dc]) in same st or sp—V-stitch made.

Begin with 29 ch.

Row 1: (right side) tr (US dc) in 5th ch from hook, *skip next 3 ch, 5 tr (US dc) in next ch, skip next 3 ch, V-st in next ch, repeat from * across.

Row 2: 3 ch (counts as first tr [US dc]), turn, 2 tr (US dc) in first 1ch sp, skip next 3 tr (US dc), V-st in next tr (US dc), *5 tr (US dc) in next 1ch sp, skip next 3 tr (US dc), V-st in next tr (US dc), repeat from * across, 3 tr (US dc) in last 1ch sp.

Row 3: 4 ch (counts as first tr [US dc] plus 1 ch), turn, tr (US dc) in same st, *5 tr (US dc) in next 1ch sp, skip next 3 tr (US dc), V-st in next tr (US dc), repeat from * across.

Repeat Rows 2 and 3 to desired size.

Do not finish off. See notes on edging.

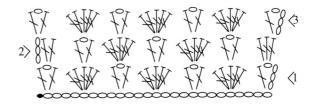

SQUARE 11: CLUSTERS

Multiples of 2 ch.

This pattern uses a 4-loop cluster.

Begin with 26 ch.

Row 1: dc (US sc) in 2nd ch from hook and in each ch across — 25 dc (US sc).

Row 2: (right side) 4 ch (counts as first tr [US dc] plus 1 ch), turn, skip next dc (US sc), *cluster in next dc (US sc), 1 ch, skip next dc (US sc), repeat from * across to last dc (US sc), tr (US dc) in last dc (US sc) — 11 clusters.

Row 3: 1 ch, turn, dc (US sc) in first tr (US dc), dc (US sc) in each 1ch sp and in each cluster across to last tr (US dc), dc (US sc) in last tr (US dc) — 25 dc (US sc).

Repeat Rows 2 and 3 to desired size.
  Do not finish off. See notes on edging.

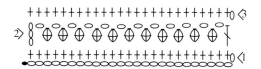

SQUARE 12: OFFSET CLUSTER

Multiples of 6 + 3 ch.

OFFSET CLUSTER:

(YO, insert hook around post of last tr [US dc] made, YO and draw up a loop, YO and draw through 2 loops) 5 times, YO and draw through all 6 loops on hook (offset cluster made).

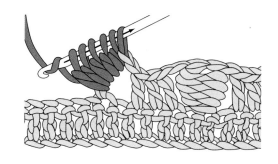

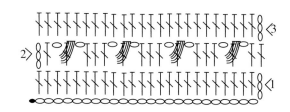

Begin with 27 ch.

Row 1: (right side) tr (US dc) in 4th ch from hook and in each ch across — 25 sts.

Row 2: 3 ch (counts as first tr [US dc], now and throughout), turn, tr (US dc) in next tr (US dc), 1 ch, skip next tr (US dc), tr (US dc) in next tr (US dc), work offset cluster around post of last tr (US dc) made, *1 ch, skip next tr (US dc), tr (US dc) in next 3 tr (US dc), 1 ch, skip next tr (US dc), tr (US dc) in next tr (US dc), offset cluster, repeat from * across to last 3 sts, 1 ch, skip next tr (US dc), tr (US dc) in next tr (US dc), tr (US dc) in top of beginning ch — 4 offset clusters.

Row 3: 3 ch, turn, tr (US dc) in next tr (US dc), tr (US dc) in first 1ch sp, tr (US dc) in top of offset cluster, tr (US dc) in next 1ch sp, *tr (US dc) in next 3 tr (US dc), tr (US dc) in 1ch sp, tr (US dc) in top of offset cluster, tr (US dc) in 1ch sp, repeat from * across to last 2 tr (US dc), tr (US dc) in last 2 tr (US dc) — 25 tr (US dc).

Repeat Rows 2 and 3 to desired size.
    Do not finish off. See notes on edging.

SQUARE 13:
SILT STITCH
Multiples of 3 ch.

Begin with 27 ch.

Row 1: (right side) tr (US dc) in 4th ch from hook and in each ch across — 25 sts.

Row 2: 1 ch, turn, (dc, 2 tr [US dc]) in first tr (US dc), skip next 2 tr (US dc), *(dc, 2 tr [US dc]) in next tr (US dc), skip next 2 tr (US dc), repeat from * across, dc in top of beginning ch — 25 sts.

Row 3: 3 ch, turn, tr (US dc) in next st and in each st across — 25 sts.

Repeat Rows 2 and 3 to desired size.
    Do not finish off. See notes on edging.

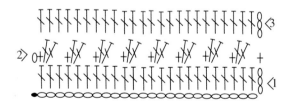

SQUARE 14:
BUSHY STITCH

Multiples of 3 + 1 ch.

Begin with 28 ch.

Row 1: (right side) (tr [US dc], 2 ch, dc [US sc]) in 4th ch from hook, *skip next 2 ch, (2 tr [US dc], 2 ch, dc [US sc]) in next ch, repeat from * across — 9 x (2 tr[US dc], 2 ch, dc [US sc]) groups.

Row 2: 2 ch, turn, (2 tr [US dc], 2 ch, dc [US sc]) in first 2ch sp and in each 2ch sp across.

Repeat Row 2 to desired size.

Do not finish off. See notes on edging.

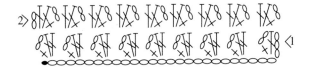

SQUARE 15:
CLUSTER BRAID CABLE

No multiple required for this pattern.

This pattern uses a Front Post cluster/FP cluster.

1. Always skip dc (US sc) behind each FP cluster and FP st throughout pattern.

2. FP sts are worked on row below dc (US sc) row.

FRONT POST CLUSTER:
(YO, insert hook around post of st indicated and pull up a loop even with hook, YO and draw through 2 loops on hook) 3 times, YO and draw through all 4 loops on hook, always skip dc (US sc) behind st just made (FP cluster made).

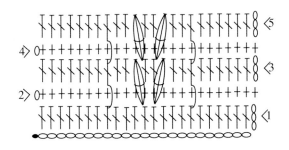

Begin with 26 ch.

Row 1: (right side) tr (US dc) in 4th ch from hook and in each ch across — 24 sts.

Row 2: 1 ch, turn, dc (US sc) in each tr (US dc) across, dc (US sc) in top of beginning ch — 24 dc (US sc).

Row 3: (*work all FP sts around tr [US dc] on row below dc [US sc] row*) 3 ch (counts as first tr [US dc], now and throughout), turn, tr (US dc) in next 6 dc (US sc), work FPtr around next tr (US dc), tr (US dc) in next 2 dc (US sc), work FP cluster around 4th tr (US dc) from last FPtr, tr (US dc) in next 2 dc (US sc), work FP cluster around next tr (US dc) (next to first cluster), tr (US dc) in next 2 dc (US sc), FPtr (US FPdc) around next tr (US dc), tr (US dc) in last 7 dc (US sc) — 24 sts.

Row 4: 1 ch, turn, dc (US sc) in each st across — 24 dc (US sc)

Row 5: (work all FP sts around tr [US dc] or FPtr [US FPdc] on row below dc (US sc) row) 3 ch, turn, tr (US dc) in next 6 dc (US sc), work FPtr (US FPdc) around next FPtr (US FPdc), tr (US dc) in next 2 dc (US sc), work FP cluster around post of tr (US dc) to left of FP cluster, tr (US dc) in next 2 dc (US sc), work FP cluster around post of next tr (US dc), tr (US dc) in next 2 dc (US sc), work FPtr (US FPdc) around next FPtr (US FPdc), tr (US dc) in next 7 dc (US sc) — 24 sts.

Repeat Rows 4 and 5 to desired size.

Do not finish off. See notes on edging.

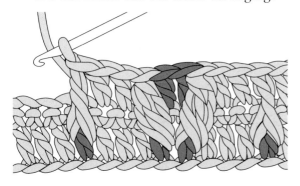

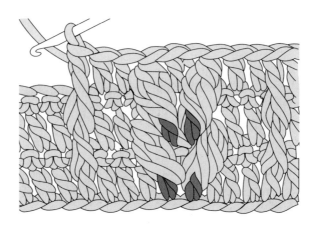

SQUARE 16: POPCORN DIAMOND

No multiple required for this pattern.

Note: 5 htr (US hdc) popcorn used in this pattern.

Begin with 26 ch.

Row 1: (right side) htr (US hdc) in 3rd ch from hook and in each ch across — 25 htr (US hdc).

Row 2: 1 ch, turn, dc (US sc) in each htr (US hdc) across, dc (US sc) in turning ch — 25 dc (US sc)

Row 3: 2 ch (counts as first htr [US hdc], now and throughout) turn, htr (US hdc) in next 11 dc

(US sc), work popcorn, htr (US hdc) in last 12 dc (US sc).

Row 4 and all wrong-side rows: 1 ch, turn, dc (US sc) in each htr (US hdc) and each popcorn across — 25 sts.

Row 5: 2 ch, turn, htr (US hdc) in next 9 dc (US sc), popcorn in next dc (US sc), htr (US hdc) in next 3 dc (US sc), popcorn in next dc (US sc), htr (US hdc) in last 10 dc (US sc).

Row 7: 2 ch, turn, htr (US hdc) in next 7 dc (US sc), popcorn in next dc (US sc), htr (US hdc) in next 7 dc (US sc), popcorn in next dc (US sc), htr (US hdc) in last 8 dc (US sc).

Row 9: 2 ch, turn, htr (US hdc) in next 5 dc (US sc), popcorn in next dc (US sc), htr (US hdc) in next 11 dc (US sc), popcorn in next dc (US sc), htr (US hdc) in last 6 dc (US sc).

Row 11: 2 ch, turn, htr (US hdc) in next 3 dc (US sc), popcorn in next dc (US sc), htr (US hdc) in next 7 dc (US sc), popcorn in next dc (US sc) twice, htr (US hdc) in last 4 dc (US sc).

Row 13: repeat Row 9.

Row 15: repeat Row 7.

Row 17: repeat Row 5.

Row 19: repeat Row 3.

Row 20: 1 ch, turn, dc (US sc) in each htr (US hdc) and each popcorn across — 25 sts.
Do not finish off. See notes on edging.

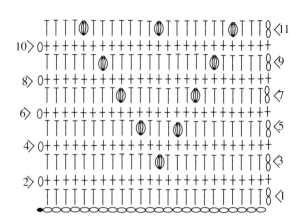

SQUARE 17:
AFGHAN 1

No multiple required for this pattern.

Begin with 5 ch, join with ss to form a ring.

Round 1: (right side) 3 ch (counts as first tr [US dc] now and throughout), 2 tr (US dc) into ring, 1 ch, (3 tr [US dc], 1 ch) 3 times, join with ss to beginning ch — 12 tr (US dc), 4 x 1ch sp.

Round 2: ss in next 2 tr (US dc) and into 1ch sp, 1 ch, (dc [US sc], 3 ch, dc [US sc], 3 ch) in same sp and in each 1ch sp around, join with ss to first dc (US sc) — 8 x 3ch sp.

Round 3: ss into first 3ch corner sp, 3 ch, (2 tr [US dc], 1 ch, 3 tr [US dc]) in same sp, 1 ch, *(3 tr [US dc] in next 3ch sp, 1 ch) across to next 3ch corner sp, (3 tr [US dc], 1 ch, 3 tr [US dc] 1 ch) in 3ch corner sp, repeat from * around, join with ss to beginning ch — 12 x 1ch sp.

Round 4: ss in next 2 tr (US dc) and into 1ch corner sp, 1 ch, *(dc [US sc], 3 ch, dc [US sc], 3 ch) in same sp, (dc [US sc] in next 1ch sp, 3 ch) across to next corner sp, repeat from * and join with ss to first dc (US sc) — 16 x 3ch sp.

Subsequent Rounds: repeat Rounds 3 and 4 alternately, finishing on Round 3, join with ss to beginning ch.

Last Round: 1 ch, dc (US sc) in same st, work 3 dc (US sc) in each corner sp, and 27 dc (US sc) across each side to next corner sp, join with ss to first dc (US sc), finish off — 120 dc (US sc).

SQUARE 18:
POPCORN BRAID CABLE
No multiple required for this pattern.

1. This pattern uses 5 tr (US dc) popcorn with 1 ch close.

2. In this pattern work FPtr (US FPdc) as follows—work FPtr (US FPdc) around the post of the tr (US dc) below the next st, always skip dc (US sc) behind FPtr (US FPdc).

Begin with 27 ch.

Row 1: (right side) tr (US dc) in 4th ch from hook and in next 8 ch, (1 ch, skip 1 ch, tr [US dc] in next ch) 3 times, tr (US dc) in each ch across — 25 sts.

Row 2: 1 ch, turn, dc (US sc) in next 10 tr (US dc), popcorn in next 1ch sp, dc (US sc) in next tr (US dc), dc (US sc) in next 1ch sp, dc (US sc) in next tr (US dc), popcorn in next 1ch sp, dc (US sc) in next 9 tr (US dc), dc (US sc) in top of beginning ch.

Row 3: 3 ch (counts as first tr [US dc], now and throughout), turn, tr (US dc) in next 5 dc (US sc), (FPtr [US FPdc] around post of tr [US dc] below next dc [US sc], tr [US dc] in next dc [US sc]) twice, 1 ch, skip popcorn, tr (US dc) in next dc (US sc), 1 ch, skip next dc (US sc), tr (US dc) in next dc (US sc), 1 ch, skip popcorn, (tr [US dc] in next dc [US sc], FPtr [US FPdc] around post of tr [US dc] below dc [US sc]) twice, tr (US dc) in last 6 dc (US sc).

Row 4: 1 ch, turn, dc (US sc) in first 10 sts, dc (US sc) in 1 ch sp, dc (US sc) in next tr (US dc), popcorn in 1 ch sp, dc (US sc) in next tr (US dc), dc (US sc) in 1 ch sp and in each st across.

Row 5: 3 ch, tr (US dc) in next 5 dc (US sc), (FPtr [US FPdc] around post of next FPtr [US FPdc], tr [US dc] in next dc [US sc]) twice, 1 ch, skip next dc (US sc), tr (US dc) in next dc (US sc), 1 ch, skip popcorn, tr (US dc) in next dc (US sc), 1 ch, skip next dc (US sc), (tr [US dc] in next dc [US sc], FPtr [US FPdc] around next FPtr [US FPdc]) twice, tr (US dc) in last 6 dc (US sc).

Row 6: 1 ch, turn, dc (US sc) in first 10 sts, popcorn in 1 ch sp, dc (US sc) in next tr (US dc), dc (US sc) in next 1 ch sp, dc (US sc) in next tr (US dc), popcorn in 1 ch sp, dc (US sc) in last 10 sts.

Row 7: 3 ch, turn, tr (US dc) in next 5 dc (US sc), (FPtr [US FPdc] around post of next FPtr [US FPdc], tr [US dc] in next dc [US sc]) twice, 1 ch, skip next popcorn, tr (US dc) in next dc (US sc), 1 ch, skip next dc (US sc), tr (US dc) in next dc (US sc), 1 ch, skip next popcorn, (tr [US dc] in next dc [US sc], FPtr [US FPdc] around next FPtr [US FPdc]) twice, tr (US dc) in last 6 dc (US sc).

Repeat Rows 4 to 7 to desired size.
    Do not finish off. See notes on edging.

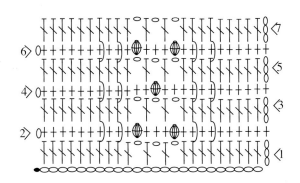

SQUARE 19:
SIMPLE SHELL STITCH
Multiples of 4 + 1 ch.

Begin with 29 ch.

Row 1: (right side) 4 tr (US dc) in 6th ch from hook, skip next 3 ch, 4 tr (US dc) in next ch, repeat across to last 3 ch, tr (US dc) in last ch — 26 sts.

Row 2: 1 ch, turn, dc (US sc) in each tr (US dc) across, dc (US sc) in top of turning ch — 26 dc (US sc).

Row 3: 3 ch (counts as first tr [US dc], now and throughout), turn, 2 tr (US dc) in first dc (US sc), *(skip next 3 dc [US sc], 4 tr [US dc] in next dc [US sc]), repeat across from * to last 5 dc (US sc), 4 tr (US dc) in last dc (US sc) — 27 tr (US dc).

Row 4: 1 ch, turn, dc (US sc) in each tr (US dc) across, dc (US sc) in top of turning ch — 27 dc (US sc).

Row 5: 3 ch, turn, skip next 2 dc (US sc), 4 tr (US dc) in next dc (US sc), skip next 3 dc (US sc), 4 tr (US dc) in next dc (US sc), repeat across to last 3 dc (US sc), tr (US dc) in last dc (US sc) — 26 tr (US dc).

Repeat Rows 2 to 5 to desired size.

Do not finish off. See notes on edging.

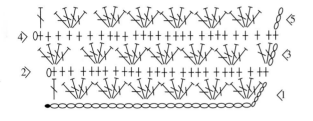

SQUARE 20:
CLIMBING SHELLS
Multiples of 10 + 7 ch.

Begin with 27 ch.

Row 1: (right side) tr (US dc) in 4th ch from hook and in next 3 ch, *skip next 2 ch, (2 tr [US dc], 2 ch, 2 tr [US dc]) in next ch (shell made), skip 2 ch, tr (US dc) in next 5 ch, repeat from * across — 2 shells.

Row 2: 3 ch (counts as first tr [US dc]), turn, tr (US dc) in next 4 tr (US dc), work shell in next 2ch sp, skip next 2 tr (US dc), tr (US dc) in next 5 tr (US dc), work shell in next 2ch sp, skip 2 tr

(US dc), tr (US dc) in next 4 tr (US dc), tr (US dc) in top of beginning ch.

Repeat Row 2 to desired size.

Do not finish off. See notes on edging.

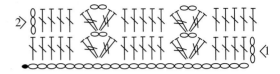

SQUARE 21:
ALIGNED SHELLS
Multiples of 6 + 3 ch.

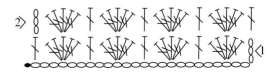

Begin with 27 ch.

Row 1: (right side) 5 tr (US dc) in 6th ch from hook, skip next 2 ch, tr (US dc) in next ch, *skip next 2 ch, 5 tr (US dc) in next ch, skip next 2 ch, tr (US dc) in next ch, repeat from * across.

Row 2: 3 ch, turn, *skip next 2 tr (US dc), 5 tr (US dc) in next tr (US dc), skip next 2 tr (US dc), tr (US dc) in next tr (US dc), repeat from * across, tr (US dc) in top of beginning ch — 25 tr (US dc).

Repeat Row 2 to desired size.

Do not finish off. See notes on edging.

SQUARE 22:
BOXED SHELL STITCH
Multiples of 5 + 4 ch.

Begin with 29 ch.

Row 1: tr (US dc) in 4th ch from hook, *3 ch, skip 3 ch, tr (US dc) in next 2 ch, repeat from * across — 5 x 3ch sp.

Row 2: (right side) 3 ch (counts as first tr [US dc], now and throughout), turn, 5 tr (US dc) in centre ch of each 3ch sp across, tr (US dc) in top of beginning ch.

Row 3: 3 ch, turn, tr (US dc) in next tr (US dc), *3 ch, skip 3 tr (US dc), tr (US dc) in next 2 tr (US dc), repeat from * across — 5 x 3ch sp.

Repeat Rows 2 and 3 to desired size.
  Do not finish off. See notes on edging.

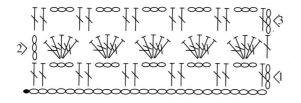

SQUARE 23:
FAN STITCH
Multiples of 10 + 7 ch.

Begin with 27 ch.

Row 1: (right side) tr (US dc) in 4th ch from hook and in next 2 ch, (htr [US hdc] in next 2 ch, dc [US sc] in next 3 ch, htr [US hdc] in next 2 ch, tr [US dc] in next 3 ch) twice, tr (US dc) in last ch — 25 sts.

Row 2: 1 ch, turn, dc (US sc) in first 4 tr (US dc), (skip next 3 sts, 7 dtr [US tr] in next dc [US sc], skip next 3 sts, dc [US sc] in next 3 tr [US dc]) twice, dc (US sc) in top of beginning ch — 25 sts.

Row 3: 3 ch (counts as first tr [US dc], now and throughout), turn, tr (US dc) in next dc (US sc) and in each st across — 25 tr (US dc).

Row 4: 3 ch, turn, tr (US dc) in next tr (US dc), 4 dtr (US tr) in next tr (US dc), skip 3 tr (US dc), dc (US sc) in next 3 tr (US dc), skip next 3 tr (US dc), 7 dtr (US tr) in next tr (US dc), skip 3 tr (US dc), dc (US sc) in next 3 tr (US dc), skip next 3 tr (US dc), 4 dtr (US tr) in next tr (US dc), tr (US dc) in last 2 tr (US dc) — 25 sts.

Row 5: 3 ch, turn, tr (US dc) in next tr (US dc) and in each st across — 25tr (US dc).

Row 6: 1 ch, turn, dc (US sc) in first 4 tr (US dc), (skip next 3 tr [US dc], 7 dtr [US tr] in next tr [US dc], skip 3 tr [US dc], dc [US sc] in next 3 tr [US dc]) twice, dc (US sc) in last tr (US dc) — 25 sts.

Repeat Rows 3 to 6 to desired size.

Do not finish off. See notes on edging.

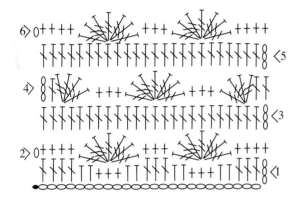

SQUARE 24:
POPCORN FAN
Multiples of 10 +6 ch.

The popcorn st in this pattern uses 5 tr (US dc) with 1 ch to close.

Begin with 26 ch.

Row 1: dc (US sc) in 2nd ch from hook and in each ch across — 25 dc (US sc).

Row 2: (right side) 3 ch (counts as first tr [US dc]), turn, tr (US dc) in next dc (US sc), popcorn, (skip 4 dc [US sc], 9 dtr [US tr] in next dc [US sc],

skip 4 dc [US sc], popcorn in next dc [US sc]) twice, tr (US dc) in last 2 dc (US sc) — 3 popcorns, 2 fans.

Row 3: 1 ch, turn, dc (US sc) in each st and popcorn across — 25 dc (US sc).

Repeat Rows 2 and 3 to desired size.

Do not finish off. See notes on edging.

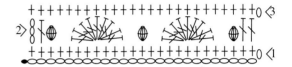

SQUARE 25:
AFGHAN 2
No multiple required for this pattern.

Begin with 5 ch, join with ss to form a ring.

Round 1: (right side) 3 ch (counts as first tr [US dc], now and throughout), 15 tr (US dc) into ring, join with ss to top of beginning ch — 16 tr (US dc).

Round 2: 4 ch (counts as 1 tr [US dc], 1 ch), *tr (US dc) in next tr (US dc), 1 ch, repeat from * around, join with ss in third ch of 4 ch — 16 tr (US dc), 16 x 1ch sp.

Round 3: ss into first 1ch sp, 3 ch (tr [US dc], 2 ch, 2 tr [US dc]) in same sp, 1 ch, htr (US hdc) in next 1ch sp, 1 ch, dc (US sc) in next 1ch sp, 1 ch, htr (US hdc) in next ch sp, 1 ch, *(2 tr [US dc], 2 ch, 2 tr [US dc] [shell made]) in next 1ch sp, 1 ch, htr [US hdc] in next 1ch sp, 1 ch, dc [US sc] in next 1ch sp, 1 ch, htr [US hdc] in next ch sp, 1 ch, repeat from * around, join with ss in first tr (US dc) — 4 x 2-ch sps — 16 x 1-ch sps — 16 x tr (US dc) — 8 x htr (US hdc) — 4 x dc (US sc)·

Round 4: ss in next tr (US dc) and into first 2ch sp, 3 ch, (tr [US dc], 2 ch, 2 tr [US dc]) in same sp, 2 ch, (htr [US hdc] in next 1ch sp, 2 ch) 4 times, *work shell in next shell, 2 ch, (htr (US hdc) in next 1ch sp, 2 ch) 4 times, repeat from * around, join with ss to first tr (US dc) — 24 x 2-ch sps — 16 x htr (US hdc) — 16 x tr (US dc)

Round 5: ss in next tr (US dc) and into first 2ch sp, 3 ch, (tr [US dc], 2 ch, 2 tr [US dc]) in same sp, (2 tr [US dc] in next 2ch sp) 5 times, *work shell in next shell, (2 tr [US dc], in next 2ch sp) 5 times, repeat from * around, join with ss to first tr (US dc) — 56 tr (US dc).

Round 6: 3 ch, tr (US dc) in next tr (US dc), (2 tr [US dc], 3 ch, 2 tr [US dc]) in first 2 ch sp, * tr (US dc) in each tr (US dc) across to next 2ch sp, (2 tr [US dc], 3 ch, 2 tr [US dc]) in next 2 ch sp, repeat from * around, join with ss to first tr (US dc) — 72 tr (US dc).

Round 7: 1 ch, dc (US sc) in same st, dc (US sc) in next 3 tr (US dc), 5 dc (US sc) in next 3ch sp, *dc (US sc) in each tr (US dc) across to next 3ch sp, 5 dc (US sc) in next 3ch sp, repeat from * around, join with ss to first dc (US sc) — 92 dc (US sc).

Round 8: 1 ch, dc (US sc) in same st, 2 dc (US sc) in next dc (US sc), dc (US sc) in next 4 dc (US sc),

3 dc (US sc) in next dc (US sc), *(dc [US sc] in next 5 dc [US sc], 2 dc [US sc] in next dc [US sc]) 3 times, dc (US sc) in next 4 dc (US sc), 3 dc (US sc) in next dc (US sc), repeat from * 2 times more, (dc [US sc] in next 5 dc [US sc], 2 dc [US sc] in next dc [US sc]) twice, dc (US sc) in last 4 dc (US sc), join with ss to first dc (US sc) — 112 dc (US sc).

Round 9: work 2nd round of edging (see beginning of chapter).

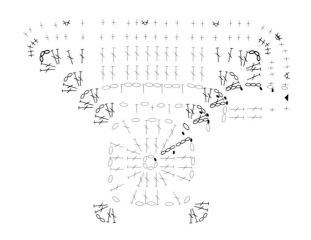

SQUARE 26: CHEQUERED SHELLS

Multiples of 4 ch.

Begin with 28 ch.

Row 1: (right side) 3 tr (US dc) in 4th ch from hook, *skip 3 ch, ss in next ch, 3 ch, 3 tr (US dc)

into same ch as ss, repeat from * to last 4 ch, skip 3 ch, dc (US sc) in last ch — 6 shells.

Row 2: 3 ch, turn, 3 tr (US dc) into first dc (US sc), *skip next 3 tr (US dc), ss into top of 3 ch of previous row, 3 ch, work 3 tr (US dc) around post of 3 ch of previous row, repeat from * to end, dc (US sc) in top of last 3 ch of previous row.

Repeat Row 2 to desired size then work one row as follows.

Last Row: 3 ch, turn, 2 tr (US dc) in first dc (US sc), *ss into top of 3 ch of previous row, 3 tr (US dc) into next ss below on previous row, repeat from * to beginning ch, dc (US sc) in top of beginning ch.

Do not finish off. See notes on edging.

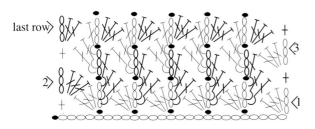

SQUARE 27: ARCH STITCH
Multiples of 5 + 3 ch.

Begin with 28 ch.

Row 1: (right side) tr (US dc) in 4th ch from hook, 2 ch, skip next 2 ch, *tr (US dc) in next 3 ch, 2 ch, skip next 2 ch, repeat from * across to last 2 ch, tr (US dc) in last 2 ch — 5 x 2ch sps.

Row 2: 1 ch, turn, dc (US sc) in first tr (US dc), skip next tr (US dc), 5 tr (US dc) in first 2 ch sp * skip next tr (US dc), dc (US sc) in next tr (US dc), skip next tr, 5 tr (US dc) in next 2-ch sp, repeat from * across, dc (US sc) in top of beginning ch.

Row 3: 4 ch, turn, skip next tr (US dc), tr (US dc) in next 3 tr (US dc), *2 ch, skip next 3 sts, tr (US dc) in next 3 tr (US dc), repeat from * across to last 2 sts, 1 ch, tr (US dc) in last dc (US sc).

Row 4: 3 ch, turn, 2 tr (US dc) in same st, skip next tr (US dc), dc (US sc) in next tr (US dc), *5 tr (US dc) in next 2ch sp, skip next tr (US dc), dc (US sc) in next tr (US dc), repeat from * across, 3 tr (US dc) in 3rd ch of beginning 4 ch.

Row 5: 3 ch, turn, tr (US dc) in next tr (US dc), 2 ch, skip next 3 sts, *tr (US dc) in next 3 tr (US dc), 2 ch, skip next 3 sts, repeat from * across to last tr (US dc), tr (US dc) in last tr (US dc), tr (US dc) in top of beginning ch.

Repeat Rows 2 to 5 to desired size.

Do not finish off. See notes on edging.

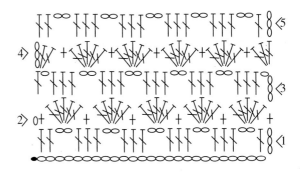

SQUARE 28:
PICOT I

Multiples of 5 ch.

Note: This pattern uses picot stitch as follows: 3 ch, dc (US sc) in 3rd ch from hook (picot made).

Begin with 30 ch.

Row 1: (right side) tr (US dc) in 4th ch from hook and in next ch, *picot, skip next 2 ch, tr (US dc) in next 3 ch, repeat from * across — 5 picots.

Row 2: 3 ch (counts as first tr [US dc], now and throughout), turn, tr (US dc) in next 2 tr (US dc), picot, *tr (US dc) in next 3 tr (US dc), picot, repeat from * across to last 3 sts, tr (US dc) in next 2 tr (US dc), tr (US dc) in top of beginning ch.

Repeat Row 2 to about 12 mm (½ in) from desired size.

Last Row: 3 ch, turn, tr (US dc) in next 2 tr (US dc), *2 ch, tr (US dc) in next 3 tr (US dc), repeat from * across.

Do not finish off. See notes on edging.

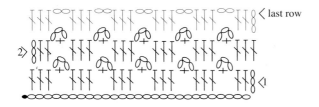

SQUARE 29:
PALMS

Multiples of 3 + 2 ch.

Begin with 26 ch.

Row 1: (right side) dc (US sc) in 2nd ch from hook, *2 ch, skip next 2 ch, dc (US sc) in next ch, repeat from * across — 8 x 2ch sp.

Row 2: 3 ch (counts as first tr [US dc]), turn, tr (US dc) in same st, 3 tr (US dc) in next dc (US sc) and in each dc (US sc) to last dc (US sc), 2 tr (US dc) in last dc (US sc) — 25 tr (US dc).

Row 3: 1 ch, turn, dc (US sc) in first tr (US dc), *2 ch, skip next 2 tr (US dc), dc (US sc) in next tr (US dc), repeat from * across — 8 x 2ch sp.

Repeat Rows 2 and 3 to desired size.
    Do not finish off. See notes on edging.

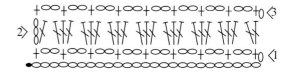

SQUARE 30:
PICOT 2

Multiples of 2 ch.

Note: picot stitch used in this pattern—3 ch, ss in 3rd ch from hook (picot made).

Begin with 26 ch.

Row 1: dc (US sc) in 2nd ch from hook and in each ch across — 25 dc (US sc).

Row 2: (right side) 1 ch, turn, dc (US sc) in first dc (US sc), *picot, skip next dc (US sc), dc (US sc) in next dc (US sc), repeat from * across — 12 picots.

Row 3: 6 ch, turn, ss in 3rd ch from hook (counts as first tr [US dc] plus picot), tr (US dc) in next dc (US sc), *picot, tr (US dc) in next dc (US sc), repeat from * across — 12 picots.

Row 4: 6 ch, turn, ss in 3rd ch from hook, tr (US dc) in next tr (US dc), *picot, tr (US dc) in next tr (US dc), repeat from * across.

Repeat Row 4 to about 12 mm (½ in) from desired size.

Next Row: 4 ch, turn, tr (US dc) in next tr (US dc), *1 ch, tr (US dc) in next tr (US dc), repeat from * across.

Last Row: 1 ch, turn, dc (US sc) in each tr (US dc) and 1ch sp across.

Do not finish off. See notes on edging.

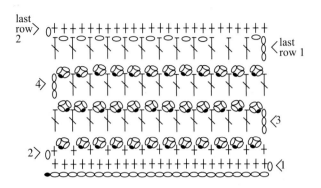

SQUARE 31:
AFGHAN 3

No multiple required for this pattern.

Note: This pattern uses beginning clusters and clusters.

Begin with 8 ch, join with ss to form ring.

Round 1: (right side) into ring work (beginning cluster, 5 ch, cluster), 2 ch, *(cluster, 5 ch, cluster), 2 ch, repeat from * twice more, join with ss to top of beginning cluster — 8 clusters.

Round 2: ss in first 5ch space, (beginning cluster, 3 ch, cluster) in same space, 2 ch, 3 tr (US dc) in next 2ch space, 2 ch, *(cluster, 3 ch, cluster) in next 5ch space, 2 ch, 3 tr (US dc) in next 2ch space, 2 ch, repeat from * around, join with ss to top of beginning cluster — 8 clusters, 12 tr (US dc).

Round 3: ss into first 3ch space, (beginning cluster, 3 ch, cluster) in same space, 2 ch, 2 tr (US dc) in next 2ch space, tr (US dc) in next 3 tr (US dc), 2 tr (US dc) in next 2ch space, 2 ch, *(cluster, 3 ch, cluster) in next 3ch sp, 2 ch, 2 tr (US dc) in next 2ch space, tr (US dc) in next 3 tr (US dc), 2 tr (US dc) in next 2ch space, 2 ch, repeat from * join with ss to top of beginning cluster — 8 clusters, 28 tr (US dc).

Rounds 4 and 5: ss into first ch space, (beginning cluster, 3 ch, cluster) in same space, 2 ch, 2 tr (US dc) in next 2ch space, tr (US dc) in each tr (US dc) across to next 2ch sp, 2 tr (US dc) in next 2ch space, 2 ch, *(cluster, 3 ch, cluster) in next 3ch sp, 2 ch, 2 tr (US dc) in next 2 ch space, tr (US dc) in each tr (US dc) across to next 2ch sp, 2 tr (US dc) in next 2ch space, 2 ch, repeat from * and join with ss to top of beginning cluster — round 4, 8 clusters, 44 tr (US dc); round 5, 8 clusters, 60 tr (US dc).

Round 6: ss into 3ch sp, 1 ch, *5 dc (US sc) in same sp, dc (US sc) in next cluster, 2 dc (US sc) in next 2ch sp, dc (US sc) in next 15 dc (US sc), 2 dc (US sc) in next 2ch sp, dc (US sc) in next cluster, repeat from * around to first dc (US sc), join with ss to first dc (US sc) — 23 dc (US sc) across, 3 dc (US sc) corner — 104 dc (US sc) total.

Do not finish off. See notes on edging — Round 1 edging: 112 dc (US sc). Round 2 edging: 120 dc (US sc).

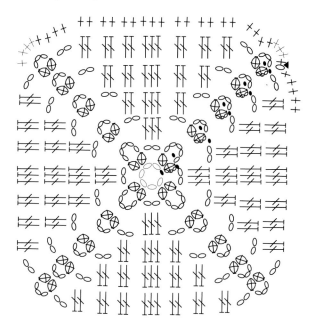

SQUARE 32:
CABLES

Multiples of 5 + 1 ch.

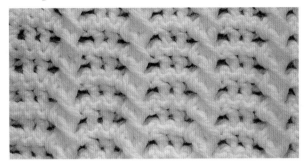

Note: Work FPtr (US FPdc) fairly loosely, draw yarn up level with hook to prevent cables curling.

Begin with 26 ch.

Row 1: (right side) tr (US dc) in 4th ch from hook and in each ch across — 24 tr (US dc).

Row 2: 1 ch, turn, dc (US sc) in each tr (US dc) across — 24 dc (US sc).

Row 3: (note: work FPtr [US FPdc] around tr [US dc] on Row 1, leaving the 3 dc [US sc] behind the FPtr [US FPdc] unused); 3 ch (counts as first tr [US dc], now and throughout), turn, *tr (US dc) in next 2 dc (US sc), skip next dc (US sc) and tr (US dc) below, work (FPtr [US FPdc] around tr [US dc] below next dc [US sc]) twice, working around both FPtr (US FPdc) just made, work FPtr (US FPdc) around skipped tr (US dc), repeat from * across to last 3 dc (US sc), tr (US dc) in last 3 dc (US sc) — 12 tr (US dc), 12 FPtr (US FPdc).

Row 4: 1 ch, turn, dc (US sc) in each st across — 24 dc (US sc).

Row 5: (note: work FPtr [US FPdc]s around FPtr [US FPdc]s on row below dc [US sc] row, skipping the 3 dc [US sc] behind the FPtr [US FPdc]s); 3 ch, turn, *tr (US dc) in next 2 dc (US sc), skip next FPtr (US FPdc), work FPtr (US FPdc) around next 2 FPtr (US FPdc), work FPtr (US FPdc) around skipped FPtr (US FPdc), repeat from * across to last 3 dc (US sc), tr (US dc) in last 3 dc (US sc) — 12 tr (US dc), 4 cables.

Repeat Rows 4 and 5 to desired size.
    Do not finish off. See notes on edging.

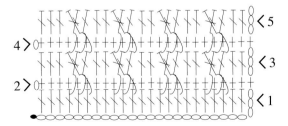

SQUARE 33:
PUFF STITCH
Multiples of 2 ch.

Note: This pattern uses a 9-loop puff with 1 ch to close.

Begin with 26 ch.

Row 1: (right side) htr (US hdc) in 3rd ch from hook and in each ch across — 25 sts.

Row 2: 3 ch (counts as first htr [US hdc] plus 1 ch, now and throughout), turn, *skip next htr (US hdc), htr (US hdc) in next htr (US hdc), 1 ch, repeat from * across to last 2 sts, skip next htr (US hdc), htr (US hdc) in top if beginning ch — 12 x 1ch sp.

Row 3: 2 ch, turn, puff st in first 1 ch sp, *1 ch, puff st in next 1ch sp, repeat from * across, htr (US hdc) in last htr (US hdc) — 12 puffs.

Row 4: 3 ch, turn, htr (US hdc) in first 1ch sp (between puffs), 1 ch, *htr (US hdc) in next 1ch sp, 1 ch, repeat from * across, htr (US hdc) in last htr (US hdc) — 12 x 1ch sp.

Row 5: 2 ch, turn, htr (US hdc) in each 1ch sp and in each htr (US hdc) across — 25 htr (US hdc).

Repeat Rows 2 to 5 to desired size.

Do not finish off. See notes on edging.

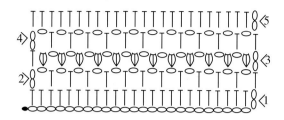

SQUARE 34:
SLANT SPIKE
Multiples of 4 + 1 ch.

SLANT SPIKE

YO, insert hook in skipped dc (US sc) and pull up a long loop (YO and draw through 2 loops on hook) twice (slant spike made).

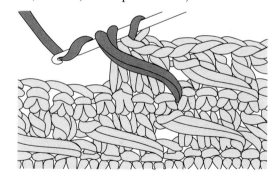

Begin with 25 ch.

Row 1: dc (US sc) in 2nd ch from hook and in each ch across — 24 dc (US sc).

Row 2: (right side) 3 ch (counts as first tr [US dc]), turn, tr (US dc) in next dc (US sc), *skip next dc (US sc), tr (US dc) in next 3 dc (US sc), work slant st in skipped dc (US sc), repeat from * across to last 2 dc (US sc), tr (US dc) in last 2 dc (US sc) — 5 slant sts.

Row 3: 1 ch, turn, dc (US sc) in each st across.

Repeat Rows 2 and 3 to desired size.
　　Do not finish off. See notes on edging.

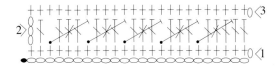

SQUARE 35:
CROSSED PUFF STITCH
Multiples of 2 + 1 ch.

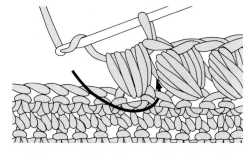

Note: 9-loop puff without 1ch close is used in this pattern.

Begin with 25 ch.

Row 1: (right side) dc (US sc) in 2nd ch from hook and in each ch across — 24 dc (US sc).

Row 2: 3 ch (counts as first tr [US dc]), turn, *skip next dc (US sc), puff in next dc (US sc), working around puff just made, work puff in skipped dc (US sc), repeat from * across to last dc (US sc), tr (US dc) in last dc (US sc) — 11 puffs.

Rows 3, 4 and 5: 1 ch, turn, dc (US sc) in each st across — 24 dc (US sc).

Repeat Rows 2 to 5 to desired size
　　Do not finish off. See notes on edging.

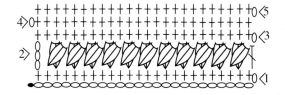

SQUARE 36:
BASKET WEAVE
Multiples of 6 +4 ch.

Note: The Post stitches in this pattern are worked in the row below.

Begin with 28 ch.

Row 1: (right side) tr (US dc) in 4th ch from hook and in each ch across — 26 sts.

Row 2: 2 ch, turn, *FPtr (US FPdc) around post of next 3 tr (US dc), BPtr (US FPdc) around next 3 tr (US dc), repeat from * across, htr (US hdc) in top of beginning ch — 26 sts.

Row 3: 2 ch, turn, *FPtr (US FPdc) around post of next 3 tr (US dc), BPtr (US FPdc) around next 3 tr (US dc), repeat from * across, htr (US hdc) in top of beginning ch — 26 sts.

Rows 4 and 5: 2 ch, turn, *BPtr (US FPdc) around post of next 3 tr (US dc), FPtr (US FPdc) around next 3 tr (US dc), repeat from * across, htr (US hdc) in top of beginning ch — 26 sts.

Row 6: repeat Row 3.

Repeat Rows 3 to 6 to desired size.
    Do not finish off. See notes on edging.

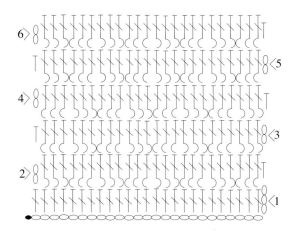

FINISHING

JOINING SQUARES

Lay out squares according to placement chart or as desired.

Pin the squares together, for easier handling working with 2 rows of squares at a time. Take care to always join from the same end for each row being joined.

Working from right to left, with right sides of both squares facing outward, work back loop (centre loops) of both squares, join in first sts using one of the joining methods listed under Techniques at the beginning of the book— invisible join (mattress stitch), visible or flat join (whip stitch), slip stitch join or dc (us sc) join. The dc (US sc) method, which is the strongest, was used for the sampler in the photo.

EDGING

Round 1: when all squares are joined, join with dc (US sc) in back loop of any corner st, 2 dc (US sc) in same st, *dc (US sc) in each st across to next corner st, 3 dc (US sc) in corner st, repeat from * around, join with ss to first dc (US sc).

Round 2: work dc (US sc) in both loops.

Repeat Rounds 1 and 2 as many times as desired.

Last Round: work crab st or reverse dc (US sc), always on the right side and in the opposite direction from usual. Join where needed, 1 ch, *insert hook into the next st on right, YO and draw up a loop, YO and draw through both loops on hook, repeat from * around.

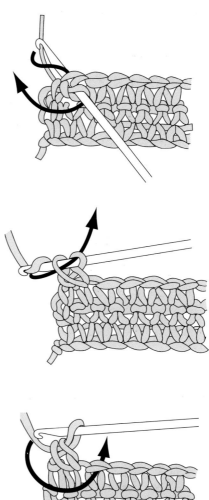

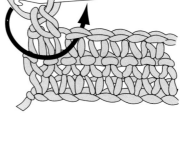

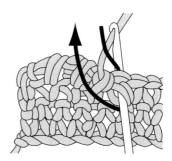

SQUARES PLACEMENT CHART

31 Afghan 3	2 Alternate puff	13 Silt	5 Cobble	10 V-stitch & shell	11 Cluster braid cable
34 Slant spike	22 Boxed shell	8 Chevron rib	19 Simple shell	16 Popcorn diamond	20 Climbing shells
9 V-stitch	36 Basket- weave	17 Afghan 1	24 Popcorn fan	11 Clusters	33 Crossed puff
1 Aligned puff	3 Alternate mesh	18 Popcorn braid cable	28 Picot 1	7 Parallel rib	14 Bushy
4 Doubles	12 Offset clusters	29 Palms	6 Horizontal rib	27 Arch	26 Chequered shells
35 Puff	30 Picot 2	32 Cables	21 Aligned Shell	23 Fan	25 Afghan 2

HEXAGON SAMPLER RUG
LEVEL: ABOVE AVERAGE TO ADVANCED

A little concentration is required for this attractive afghan but it adds another 19 stitches to your repertoire.

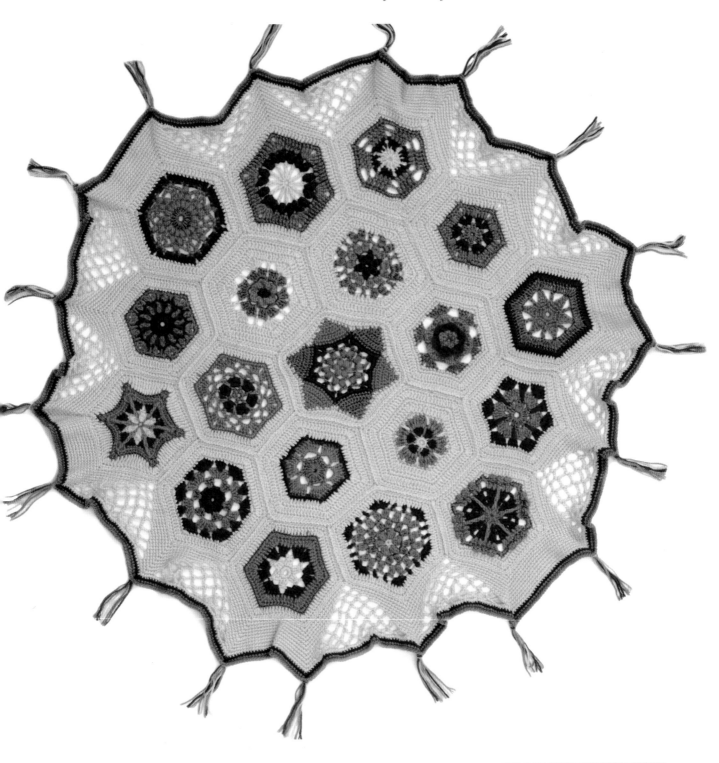

REQUIREMENTS For the rug in the photo I used a 4.50 (US G) crochet hook and Patons Zhivago 8-ply wool—approximately 100 g each of Magenta, Olive Green and Orange for Cols 1, 2 and 3, and 400 g of Off-White for Col-4.

FINISHING INDIVIDUAL MOTIFS

As you complete each motif finish it with the three rounds of edging below, following the instructions for either continuing yarn or joining new yarn as specified in the particular pattern.

Continuing yarn

Round A: 1 ch, dc (US sc) in same st or sp, *dc (US sc) in each st across to corner, 3 dc (US sc) in corner sp, repeat from * around, join with ss to first dc (US sc).

Round B: 3 ch, *tr (US dc) in each st across to corner, 3 tr (US dc) in corner st, repeat from * around, join with ss in top of beginning ch.

Round C: 1 ch, dc (US sc) in same st, * dc (US sc) in each st or sp across to corner st or sp, 3 dc (US sc) in corner st or sp, repeat from * around, join with ss in first dc (US sc).

Joining new yarn

Round A: Join with dc (US sc) in any corner st or sp, 2 dc (US sc) in same st or sp, *dc (US sc) in each st across to corner, 3 dc (US sc) in corner sp, repeat from * around, join with ss to first dc (US sc). Finish off *only if changing colour*—otherwise go on to round B. Count 13 sts across each side, one st in each corner — 84 dc (US sc) total.

Round B: 3 ch in any corner st or sp, 2 tr (US dc) in same st, *tr (US dc) in each st across to corner, 3 tr (US dc) in corner st, repeat from * around, join with ss in top of beginning ch. Finish off *only if changing colour*—otherwise go on to round C. Count 15 sts across each side, one st in each corner — 96 tr (US dc) total.

Round C: join with dc (US sc) in any corner st or sp, 2 dc (US sc) in same st or sp, *dc (US sc) in each st or sp across to corner st or sp, 3 dc (US sc) in corner st or sp, repeat from * around, join with ss in first dc (US sc), finish off. Count 17 sts across each side, one st in each corner — 108 dc (US sc) total.

ABBREVIATIONS

ch	chain
ss	slip stitch
dc (US sc)	double crochet (US single crochet)
tr (US dc)	treble (US double crochet)
htr (US hdc)	half treble (US half double crochet)
dtr (US tr)	double treble (US treble)
trtr (US dtr)	triple treble (US double treble)
qtr (US trtr)	quadruple treble (US triple treble)
BPtr (US BPdc)	Back Post treble (US Back Post double crochet)
FPtr (US FPdc)	Front Post treble (US Front Post double crochet)
FPhtr (US FPhdc)	Front Post half treble (US Front Post half double crochet)
YO	yarn over
sp	space
st	stitch

HEXAGON DIAGRAM SYMBOLS

○ = chain ch

● = slip stitch ss/sl st

+ = double crochet (US single crochet) dc (US sc)

T = half treble (US half double crochet) htr (US hdc)

⌡ = treble (US double crochet) tr (US dc)

⌡ = double treble (US treble) dtr (US tr)

⌡ = triple treble (US double treble) trtr (US dtr)

⌡ = quadruple treble (US triple treble) qtr (US trtr)

⌡ ⌠ ⊢ = work in back loops
a   b   c

⌡ ⌠ ⊢ = work in front loops
a   b   c

⌡ ⌡ ⌡ ⌡ ᕑ ᕑ ᕑ = back post BPtr (US BPdc)
a b c d e f g   BPhtr (US BPhdc) BPdc
                 (US BPsc) BPss

ᕑ ᕑ ᕑ ᕑ ᕑ ᕑ ᕑ = front post FPtr (US FPdc)
a b c d e f g   FPhtr (US FPhdc) FPdc
                 (US FPsc) FPss

Λ Λ A = decrease
a   b   c

◀ = finish off

◁ = bring in new yarn/colour

⌒ = unused ch

⟨ ⟩ = row turn

◊ ◊ = puff stitch
a b

= beginning clusters
a   b   c   d

= clusters foundation one stitch cluster (FOSC)
a   b   c   d   e   f

= one stitch cluster (OSC)

= beginning popcorns

= popcorns
a   b   c

= wrap or offset stitch

= bullions with number of wraps

= long or spike stitch
a   b   c

⊠ = reverse dc (US sc) (crab st)

⊠ = reverse dc (US sc) (crab st) in front loop

STITCH GUIDE

Joining with dc (US sc): when asked to join with a dc (US sc), begin with a slip knot on hook. Insert hook into stitch or space indicated, YO and pull up loop, YO and draw through both loops on hook.

Decrease: uses more than one st as indicated in pattern.

tr (US dc) decrease: *YO, insert hook in next tr (US dc), YO and pull up a loop, YO and draw through 2 loops on hook, repeat from * for the number of sts required to decrease, draw through all loops on hook to make one st.

dc (US sc) decrease: *insert hook in next dc (US sc), YO and pull up a loop, repeat from * for the number of sts required to decrease, draw through all loops on hook to make one st.

Long double crochet/Ldc (US long single crochet/Lsc): insert hook in st indicated, YO and pull up a loop even with loop on hook, YO and draw through both loops on hook.

Long treble/Ltr (US long double crochet/Ldc): YO, insert hook in st or sp indicated, YO and pull up a loop even with loop on hook, (YO and draw through 2 loops on hook) twice.

Double treble/dtr (US treble/tr): YO twice, insert hook in st or sp indicated, YO and pull up a loop (4 loops on hook), (YO and draw through 2 loops) 3 times.

Triple treble/trtr (US double treble/dtr): YO 3 times, insert hook in st or sp indicated, YO and pull up a loop (5 loops on hook), (YO and draw through 2 loops) 3 times.

Quadruple treble/qtr (US triple treble/trtr): YO 4 times, insert hook in st or sp indicated, YO and pull up a loop (6 loops on hook), (YO and draw through 2 loops) 5 times.

 Beginning popcorn: the beginning 3 ch for tr (US dc) and 2 ch for htr (US hdc) always counts as the first tr (US dc) or htr (US hdc).

  Beginning cluster: the beginning 3 ch for tr (US dc) and 2 ch for htr (US hdc) always counts as the first tr (US dc) or htr (US hdc).

Long cluster/LC: YO, working around next st or sp, insert hook into st or sp on row or round below, YO and pull up a loop even with last st made, YO and draw through 2 loops on hook, YO, insert hook into same st or sp, YO and pull up a loop even with last st made, YO and draw through all 3 loops on hook.

One stitch cluster/OSC: uses one ch, st or sp as pattern indicates. 3 ch, YO, insert hook in 3rd ch from hook, YO and pull up a loop, YO and draw through 2 loops on hook, YO, insert hook in same ch, YO and pull up a loop, YO and draw through 2 loops on hook, YO and draw through all 3 loops on hook.

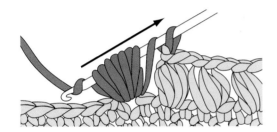 **Front Post double treble/FPdtr (US Front post treble/FPtr):** YO twice, insert hook from front to back around post of st indicated, YO and draw up a loop (4 loops on hook), YO and draw through 2 loops on hook) 3 times.

Puff stitch: (YO, insert hook in st or space, YO and pull up a loop even with hook) 3 or 4 times, YO and draw through all 7 or 9 loops on hook, 1 ch to close.

MOTIF I

Assign Col-1, Col-2, Col-3 to the colours of your choice.

Begin with (Col-1) 5 ch, join with ss to form a ring.

Round 1: (right side) 3 ch, into ring work (2 tr [US dc], 1 ch) once and then (3 tr [US dc], 1 ch) 5 times more, join with ss to beginning ch, finish off — 6 shells, 6 x 1ch sp.

Round 2: (Col-2) join with ss in any 1ch sp, 3 ch, 2 tr (US dc), 3 ch in same sp, *3 tr (US dc), 3 ch in next 1ch sp, repeat from * around, join with ss to beginning ch, finish off — 6 shells, 6 x 3ch sp.

Round 3: (Col-3) join with ss in any 3ch sp, 3 ch, 2 tr (US dc), 1 ch, 3 tr (US dc) in same sp, 1 ch, *3 tr (US dc), 1 ch, 3 tr (US dc) in next 3ch sp, 1 ch, repeat from * around, join with ss to beginning ch, finish off — 12 shells, 12 x 1ch sp.

Round 4: (Col-1) join with ss in any corner sp, 3 ch, 2 tr (US dc), 1 ch, 3 tr (US dc) in same sp, 1 ch, 3 tr (US dc) in next 1ch sp, 1 ch, *3 tr (US dc), 1 ch, 3 tr (US dc) in next corner sp, 1 ch, 3 tr (US dc) in next 1ch sp, 1 ch, repeat from * around, join with ss to beginning ch, finish off — 18 shells, 18 x 1ch sp.

Rounds 5, 6 and 7: See Finishing individual motifs, Joining new yarn A, and Continuing yarn B and C (Col-4).

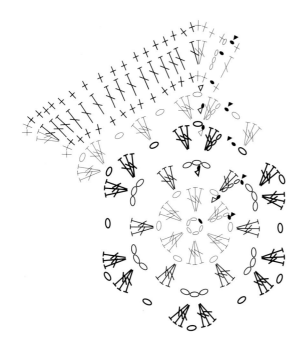

MOTIF 2

Assign Col-1, Col-2, Col-3 to the colours of your choice.

Begin with (Col-2) 4 ch.

Round 1: (Col-2) into 4th ch from hook work (2 tr [US dc], 1 ch) once, and then (3 tr [US dc], 1 ch) 5 times, join with ss in 3rd ch of beginning ch, finish off — 6 shells, 6 x 1ch sp.

Round 2: (Col-3) join with ss in any 1ch sp, 5 ch, *(ss in next 1ch sp, 5 ch), repeat from * around, join with ss to first ss, do not finish off — 6 x 5ch sp.

Round 3: ss into first 5ch sp, 3 ch (counts as first tr [US dc], now and throughout), (3 tr [US dc], 2 ch, 4 tr [US dc]) in same sp, 1 ch, *(4 tr [US dc], 2 ch, 4 tr [US dc]) in next 5ch sp, 1 ch, repeat from * around, join with ss to beginning ch, finish off — 48 tr (US dc), 6 x 2ch sps, 6 x 1ch sp.

Round 4: (Col-1) join with dc (US sc) in any corner sp, 1 ch, dc (US sc) in same sp, dc (US sc) in next 3 tr (US dc), skip next tr (US dc), (dc [US sc], 1 ch, dc [US sc]) in 1ch sp, skip next tr (US dc), dc (US sc) in next 3 tr (US dc), *(dc [US sc], 1 ch, dc [US sc]) in next corner sp, dc (US sc) in next 3 tr (US dc), skip next tr (US dc), (dc [US sc], 1 ch, dc [US sc]) in 1ch sp, skip next tr (US dc), dc (US sc) in next 3 tr (US dc), repeat from * around, join with ss in first dc (US sc), finish off — 66 sts.

Round 5: (Col-4) join with ss in any corner sp, 3 ch, (tr [US dc], 1 ch, 2 tr [US dc]) in same st, 9 tr (US dc) across to next corner, *(2 tr [US dc], 1 ch, 2 tr [US dc]) in corner space, 9 tr (US dc) across to next corner, repeat from * around, join with ss to beginning ch, do not finish off — 84 tr (US dc).

Rounds 6 and 7: See Finishing individual motifs, Continuing yarn B and C (Col-4).

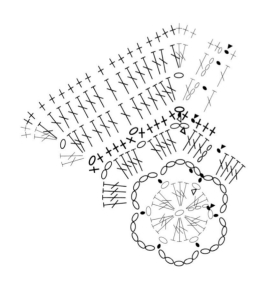

MOTIF 3

Assign Col-1, Col-2, Col-3 to the colours of your choice.

Begin with (Col-4) 4 ch, join with ss to form a ring.

Round 1: into ring work 3 ch, tr (US dc), 2 ch, and (2 tr [US dc], 2 ch) 5 times, join with ss to beginning ch, finish off — 12 tr (US dc), 6 x 2ch sp.

Round 2: (Col-1) join with ss in 2ch sp before last tr (US dc) made, 3 ch, tr (US dc) in next 2 tr (US dc), 2 ch, *tr (US dc) in next 2ch sp before next tr (US dc), tr (US dc) in next 2 tr (US dc), 2 ch, repeat from * around, join with ss to beginning ch, finish off — 18 tr (US dc), 6 x 2ch sp.

Round 3: (Col-3) join with ss in 2ch sp before last tr (US dc) made, 3 ch, tr (US dc) in next 3 tr (US dc), 3 ch, *tr (US dc) in next 2ch sp before next tr (US dc), tr (US dc) in next 3 tr (US dc), 3 ch, repeat from * around, join with ss to beginning ch, finish off — 24 tr (US dc), 6 x 3ch sp.

Round 4: (Col-2) join with ss in 3ch sp before last tr (US dc) made, 3 ch, tr (US dc) in next 4 tr (US dc), 4 ch, *tr (US dc) in next 3ch sp before next tr (US dc), tr (US dc) in next 4 tr (US dc), 4 ch, repeat from * around, join with ss to beginning ch, do not finish off — 30 tr (US dc), 6 x 4ch sp.

Round 5: 1 ch, dc (US sc), 2 ch, dc [US sc]) in same tr (US dc), dc (US sc) in next 4 tr (US dc), 5 dc (US sc) in next 4ch sp, *(dc [US sc], 2 ch, dc [US sc]) in next tr (US dc), dc (US sc) in next 4 tr (US dc), 5 dc (US sc) in next 4ch sp, repeat from * around, join with ss to first dc (US sc), finish off — 66 dc (US sc), 6 x 2ch sp.

Rounds 6, 7 and 8: See Finishing individual motifs, Joining new yarn A, Continuing yarn B and C (Col-4).

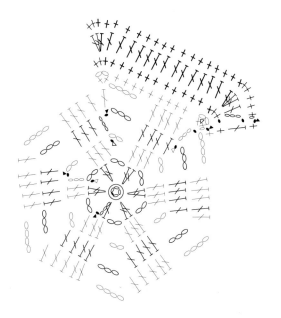

MOTIF 4

Long treble/Ltr (US long double crochet/Ldc)

Assign Col-1, Col-2, Col-3 to the colours of your choice.

Begin with (Col-2) 5 ch, join with ss to form a ring.

Round 1: 3 ch (counts as first tr [US dc], now and throughout), 2 tr (US dc), 2 ch, *3 tr (US dc), 2 ch, repeat from * 5 times, join with ss in top of beginning ch, finish off — 18 tr (US dc), 6 x 2ch sp.

Round 2: (Col-3) join with ss in any 2ch sp, 3 ch, 2 tr (US dc), 2 ch, 3 tr (US dc), in same sp, 2 ch, *(3 tr [US dc], 2 ch, 3 tr [US dc]) in next 2ch sp, 2 ch, repeat from * around, join with ss in top of beginning ch, finish off — 36 tr (US dc), 12 x 2ch sp.

Round 3: (note: work Ltr [US Ldc] into 2nd tr [US dc] of Round 1, working Ltr [US Ldc] loosely) (Col-1) join with ss in any corner sp, 3 ch, 2 tr (US dc), 2 ch, 3 tr (US dc), in same sp, 1 ch, work (tr [US dc], Ltr [US Ldc], tr [US dc]) in next 2ch sp, 1 ch, *(3 tr [US dc], 2 ch, 3 tr [US dc]) in next 2ch sp, 1 ch, work (tr [US dc], Ltr [US Ldc], tr [US dc]) in next 2 ch sp, 1 ch, repeat from * around, join with ss in top of beginning ch, finish off — 48 tr (US dc), 6 Ltr (US Ldc).

Rounds 4, 5 and 6: See Finishing individual motifs, Joining new yarn A, and Continuing yarn B and C (Col-4).

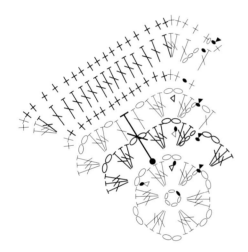

MOTIF 5

Beginning popcorn uses 3 ch, 3 tr (US dc).

Popcorn uses 4 tr (US dc).

Assign Col-1, Col-2, Col-3 to the colours of your choice.

Begin with (Col-4) 5 ch, join with ss to form a ring.

Round 1: 7 ch (counts as 1 dtr [US tr] and 3 ch), then into ring work (dtr [US tr], 3 ch) 11 times, join with ss to 4th ch of beginning ch, finish off — 12 dtr (US tr), 12 x 3ch sp.

Round 2: (Col-1) join with ss in any 3ch sp, beginning popcorn, 3 ch, popcorn in same sp, 3 ch, popcorn into next 3ch sp, 3 ch, *(popcorn, 3 ch, popcorn) into next 3ch sp, 3 ch, popcorn into next 3ch sp, repeat from * around, join with ss to top of beginning popcorn, finish off — 18 popcorns.

Round 3: (Col-3) join with ss in any corner sp, 4 ch, 2 dtr (US tr), 2 ch, 3 dtr (US tr) in same sp, 2 htr (US hdc) in next 3ch sp, htr (US hdc) in top of popcorn, 2 htr (US hdc) in next 3ch sp, *(3 dtr [US tr], 2 ch, 3 dtr [US tr]) in next corner sp, 2 htr (US hdc) in next 3ch sp, htr (US hdc) in top of popcorn, 2 htr (US hdc) in next 3ch sp, repeat from * around, join with ss to beginning ch, finish off — 36 dtr (US tr), 30 htr (US hdc), 66 sts total.

Round 4: (Col-2) join with dc (US sc) in any corner sp, 2 dc (US sc) in same sp, FPdc (US FPsc) around next 3 dtr (US tr), FPtr (US FPdc) around next 5 htr (US hdc), *FPdc (US FPsc) around next 3 dtr (US tr), 3 dc (US sc) in corner sp, FPdc (US FPsc) around next 3 dtr (US tr), FPtr (US FPdc) around next 5 htr (US hdc), repeat from * to last 3 dtr (US tr), FPdc (US FPsc) around last 3 dtr (US tr), join with ss to first dc (US sc), finish off — 84 sts.

Rounds 5 and 6: See Finishing individual motifs, Joining new yarn B, and Continuing yarn C (Col-4).

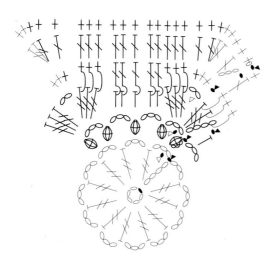

MOTIF 6

For this pattern work clusters as follows, noting that both beginning cluster and cluster use next 2 dc (US sc).

Beginning cluster: 2 ch, *YO, insert hook in next dc (US sc), YO and pull up a loop, YO and draw through 2 loops on hook, repeat from * once more, YO and draw through all 3 loops on hook.

Cluster: YO, insert hook in same st, YO and pull up a loop, YO and draw through 2 loops, *YO, insert hook in next dc (US sc), YO and pull up a loop, YO and draw through 2 loops, repeat from * once more, YO and draw through all 4 loops on hook.

Assign Col-1, Col-2, Col-3 to the colours of your choice.

Begin with (Col-4) 5 ch, join with ss to form a ring.

Round 1: 1 ch, 12 dc (US sc) in ring, join with ss to first dc (US sc), do not finish off.

Round 2: work beginning cluster, 4 ch, (work cluster, 4 ch) around, working last leg of last cluster in same st as beginning cluster, join with ss in top of first cluster, finish off — 6 clusters, 6 x 4ch sp.

Round 3: (Col-1) join with ss in any 4ch sp, (3 ch, 2 tr [US dc], 2 ch, 3 tr [US dc]) in same sp, 1 ch, *(3 tr [US dc], 2 ch, 3 tr [US dc], 1 ch) in each 4ch sp, repeat from * around, join with ss in top of beginning ch, finish off — 36 tr (US dc).

Round 4: (Col-3) join with ss in any corner sp, (3 ch, 1 tr [US dc], 1 ch, 2 tr [US dc]) in same sp, tr (US dc) in each tr (US dc) and 1ch sp to next corner sp, *(2 tr [US dc], 1 ch, 2 tr [US dc]) in corner sp, tr (US dc) in each tr (US dc) and 1ch sp to next corner sp, repeat from * around, join with ss in top of beginning 3 ch, finish off – 66 tr (US dc).

Round 5: See Finishing individual motifs with col-2, Joining new yarn A.

Rounds 6 and 7: See Finishing individual motifs, Joining new yarn B, and Continuing yarn C (Col-4).

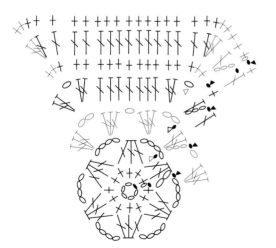

MOTIF 7

Beginning cluster uses 3 ch, 3 tr (US dc).

Cluster uses 4 tr (US dc).

Ldc (US Lsc) on Round 3 is worked in both loops of tr (US dc) of Round 1.

Assign Col-1, Col-2, Col-3 to the colours of your choice.

Begin with (Col-2) 5 ch, join with ss to form a ring.

Round 1: 5 ch (counts as tr [US dc] plus 2 ch) into ring, work tr (US dc), 2 ch, tr (US dc), 2 ch, 5 times, join with ss to 3rd ch of beginning ch, finish off — 6 tr (US dc), 6 x 2ch sp.

Round 2: (Col-1) join with ss in any 2ch sp, beginning cluster, 4 ch, *cluster in next 2ch sp, 4 ch, repeat from * around, join with ss to beginning cluster, finish off — 6 clusters, 6 x 4ch sp.

Round 3: (see diagram above for Ldc [US Lsc] in this round) (Col-3) join with dc (US sc) in top of any cluster, 3 ch, work Ldc (US Lsc), 3 ch, *dc (US sc) in next cluster, 3 ch, Ldc (US Lsc), 3 ch, repeat from * around, join with ss in first dc (US sc), do not finish off — 12 x 3ch sp.

Round 4: ss into next 2 chs, 1 ch, dc (US sc) in same 3ch sp, 4 ch, *(dc [US sc] in next 3ch sp, 4 ch), repeat from * around, join with ss to first dc (US sc), do not finish off — 12 x 4ch sp.

Round 5: ss into next 2 ch, 1 ch, dc (US sc) in same 4ch sp, 2 ch, *(3 tr [US dc], 2 ch, 3 tr [US dc]) into next 4ch sp, 2 ch, dc (US sc) in next 4ch sp, 2 ch, repeat from * around, join with ss to first dc (US sc), do not finish off — 36 tr (US dc), 6 dc (US sc).

Round 6: 1 ch, dc (US sc) in same st, 2 dc (US sc) in next 2ch sp, *dc (US sc) in next 3 tr (US dc), 3 dc (US sc) in corner sp, dc (US sc) in next 3 tr (US dc), 2 dc (US sc) in next 2ch sp, dc (US sc) in next dc (US sc), 2 dc (US sc) in next 2ch sp, repeat from * around, join with ss to first dc (US sc), finish off — 84 dc (US sc).

Rounds 7 and 8: See Finishing individual motifs, Joining new yarn B, and Continuing yarn C (Col-4).

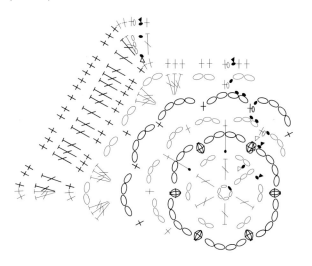

MOTIF 8

Assign Col-1, Col-2, Col-3 to the colours of your choice.

Begin with (Col-3) 5 ch, join with ss to form a ring.

Round 1: 1 ch, 18 dc (US sc) in ring, join with ss to first dc (US sc), do not finish off.

Round 2: 5 ch (worked loosely), dc (US sc) in 2nd dc (US sc) from hook, htr (US hdc) in next ch, tr (US dc) in next ch, dtr (US tr) in last ch, skip next 2 dc (US sc), ss in next dc (US sc), *5 ch, dc (US sc) in 2nd dc (US sc) from hook, htr (US hdc) in next ch, tr (US dc) in next ch, dtr (US tr) in last ch, skip next 2 dc (US sc), ss in next dc (US sc), repeat from * around, finish off — 6 points.

Round 3: (Col-2) (work dtr [US tr] in ss at base of point), join with ss in top of any point, 3 ch, dtr (US tr), 3 ch, *ss in top st of point, 3 ch, dtr (US tr), 3 ch, repeat from * around, ss to first ss, do not finish off — 6 dtr (US tr), 12 x 3ch sp.

Round 4: 3 ch, 1 tr (US dc), 2 ch, 2 tr (US dc), in same st, 3 tr (US dc) in next 3ch sp, tr (US dc) in next tr (US dc), 3 tr (US dc) in next 3ch sp, *(2 tr [US dc], 2 ch, 2 tr [US dc]) in next corner sp, 3 tr (US dc) in next 3ch sp, tr (US dc) in next tr (US dc), 3 tr (US dc) in next 3 ch sp, join with ss in beginning ch, finish off — 66 tr (US dc), 6 x 2ch sp.

Round 5: (Col-1) join with ss in any 2ch sp, 2 ch, 2 htr (US hdc) in same sp, 11 htr (US hdc) across to next corner sp, *3 htr (US hdc) in corner, 11 htr (US hdc) across to next corner sp, repeat from * around, join with ss in beginning ch, finish off — 84 htr (US hdc).

Rounds 6 and 7: See Finishing individual motifs, Joining new yarn B, and Continuing yarn C (Col-4).

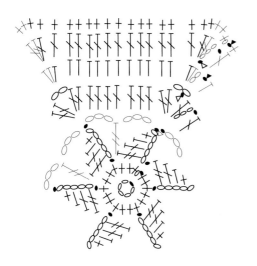

MOTIF 9

Decrease: in this pattern use next 2 tr (US dc).

Front Post triple treble/FPTrtr (US FP dtr): is worked around first tr (US dc) and then every 2nd tr (US dc) on Round 1, always skipping decrease on Round 3.

One stitch cluster/OSC: see Stitch guide for this sampler.

Assign Col-1, Col-2, Col-3 to the colours of your choice.

Begin with (Col-3) 4 ch.

Round 1: (Col-3) work 11 tr (US dc) in 4th ch from hook, join with ss to beginning ch, finish off — 12 tr (US dc).

Round 2: (Col-1) join with ss in same st as joining st, 3 ch (counts as first tr [US dc] now and throughout), tr (US dc) in same st, 2 tr (US dc) in next tr (US dc), 1 ch, *2 tr (US dc) in each of next 2 tr (US dc), 1 ch, repeat from * around, join with ss to beginning ch, do not finish off — 24 tr (US dc), 6 x 1ch sp.

Round 3: 3 ch, tr (US dc) in same st, decrease, 2 tr (US dc) in next tr (US dc), 2 ch, *2 tr (US dc) in next tr (US dc), decrease, 2 tr (US dc) in next tr (US dc), 2 ch, repeat from * around, join with ss to beginning ch, finish off — 24 tr (US dc), 6 decreases, 6 x 2ch sp.

Round 4: (Col-3) join with ss in same st as joining st, 3 ch, tr (US dc) in same st *and* in next tr (US dc), work FPtrtr (US dtr), tr (US dc) in next tr (US dc), 2 tr (US dc) in next tr (US dc), 2 ch, *2 tr (US dc) in next tr (US dc), tr (US dc) in next tr (US dc), work FPtrtr (US dtr), tr (US dc) in next tr (US dc), 2 tr (US dc) in next tr (US dc), 2 ch, repeat from * around, join with ss to beginning ch, finish off — 36 tr (US dc), 6 x 2 ch sp, 6 FPTrtr (US dtr).

Round 5: (Col-2) join with dc (US sc) in any corner sp, (1 dc [US sc], 2 ch, 2 dc [US sc] in same sp), *dc (US sc) in next tr (US dc), (ss into next tr [US dc], work OSC in same st as ss, dc [US sc] in next tr [US dc]) 3 times, (2 dc [US sc],

2 ch, 2 dc [US sc]) in next corner sp, repeat from * around, join with ss in first dc (US sc), finish off — 18 OSC, 6 x 2ch sp.

Round 6: (work behind OSC) (Col-4) (count 13 dc [US sc] across each side, not including corner st), join with dc (US sc) in any corner sp, 2 dc (US sc) in same sp, dc (US sc) in each dc (US sc) and ss across to next corner st, *3 dc (US sc) in corner sp, dc (US sc) in each dc (US sc) and ss across to next corner st, repeat from * around, do not finish off — 84 dc (US sc).

Rounds 7 and 8: See Finishing individual motifs, Continuing yarn B and C (Col-4).

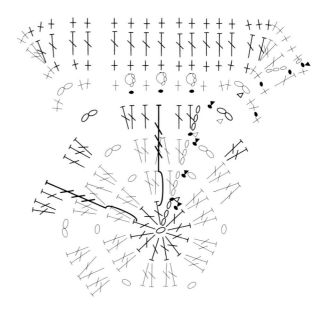

MOTIF 10

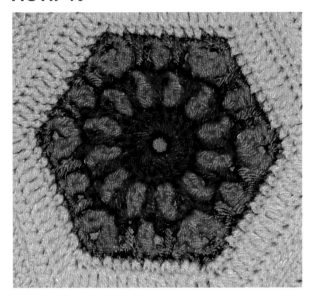

⊕ Beginning cluster uses 2 ch, 1 tr (US dc)

⊖ Cluster uses 2 tr (US dc)

Long double crochet/Ldc (US Lsc): see Stitch guide for this sampler.

Assign Col-1, Col-2, Col-3 to the colours of your choice.

Begin with (Col-1) 5 ch, join with ss to form a ring.

Round 1: 3 ch, 23 tr (US dc) in ring, join with ss to beginning ch, finish off — 24 tr (US dc).

Round 2: (Col-3) join with ss in any tr (US dc), beginning cluster in same tr (US dc), 3 ch, skip next tr (US dc), *cluster in next tr (US dc), 3 ch, skip next tr (US dc), repeat from * around, join with ss to top of beginning cluster, finish off — 12 clusters, 12 x 3ch sp.

Round 3: (note Ldc [US Lsc] uses the skipped tr [US dc] on Round 1) (Col-1) join with dc (US sc) in any 3ch sp, work Ldc (US Lsc), dc (US sc) in same 3ch sp, 2 ch, *(dc [US sc], Ldc [US Lsc], dc [US sc]) in next 3ch sp, 2 ch, repeat from * around, join with ss in first dc (US sc), finish off — 12 Ldc (US Lsc), 24 dc (US sc), 12 x 2ch sp.

Round 4: (Col-3) join with ss in any Ldc (US Lsc), (beginning cluster, 2 ch, cluster) in same st, 2 ch, cluster in next Ldc (US Lsc), 2 ch, *(cluster, 2 ch, cluster) in next Ldc (US Lsc), 2 ch, repeat from * around, join with ss in top of beginning cluster, finish off — 18 Clusters, 18 x 2ch sp.

Round 5: (Ldc [US Lsc] is worked around 2 ch sp on Round 3) (Col-2) join with dc (US sc) in any corner sp, 2 dc (US sc) in same sp, 1 ch, (dc [US sc], Ldc [US Lsc], dc [US sc] in next 2ch sp, 1 ch) twice, *3 dc (US sc) in corner sp, 1 ch, (dc [US sc], Ldc [US Lsc], dc [US sc] in next 2ch sp, 1 ch) twice, repeat from * around, join with ss to first dc (US sc), finish off — 12 Ldc (US Lsc), 42 dc (US sc), 18 x 1ch sp.

Round 6: (Col-4) join with dc (US sc) in any corner st, 2 dc (US sc) in same st, *dc (US sc) in each st across to next corner st, 3 dc (US sc) in corner st, repeat from * around, join with ss in first dc (US sc), do not finish off — 84 dc (US sc).

Rounds 7 and 8: See Finishing individual motifs, Continuing yarn, B and C (Col-4).

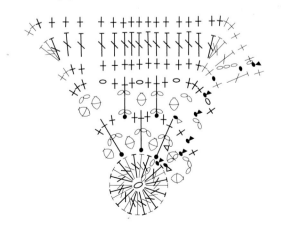

MOTIF 11

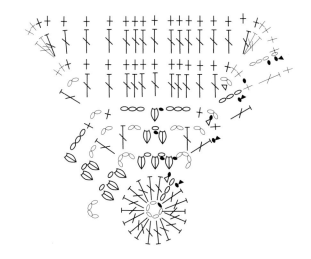 **Puff** uses 7 loops on hook.

Assign Col-1, Col-2, Col-3 to the colours of your choice.

Begin with (Col-2) 5 ch, join with ss to form a ring.

Round 1: 3 ch, 17 tr (US dc) into ring, join with ss to beginning ch, finish off — 18 tr (US dc).

Round 2: (work in sp between tr [US dc]) (Col-3) join with ss in any sp between tr (US dc), puff in same sp, 1 ch, puff in next sp, 1 ch, puff in next sp, 4 ch, *(puff in next sp, 1 ch) twice, puff in next sp, 4 ch, repeat from * around, join with ss to first puff, do not finish off — 18 puffs, 6 x 4ch sp, 12 x 1ch sp.

Round 3: ss into next 1ch sp, puff in same sp, 1 ch, puff in next 1ch sp, 2 ch, (tr [US dc], 2 ch, tr [US dc]) in next 4ch sp, 2 ch, *puff in next 1ch sp, 1 ch, puff in next 1ch sp, 2 ch, (tr [US dc], 2 ch, tr [US dc]) in next 4ch sp, 2 ch, repeat from * around, join with ss to first puff, do not finish

off — 12 puffs, 12 tr (US dc), 6 x 1ch sp, 18 x 2ch sp.

Round 4: ss into next 1ch sp, puff in same sp, 3 ch, skip next 2ch sp *and* next tr (US dc), (dc [US sc], 2 ch, dc [US sc]) in next 2ch sp, 3 ch, skip next tr (US dc) *and* next 2ch sp, *puff in next ch sp, skip next 2ch sp *and* next tr (US dc), (dc [US sc], 2 ch, dc [US sc]) in next 2ch sp, 3 ch, skip next 2ch sp *and* next tr (US dc), repeat from * around, join with ss to first puff, finish off — 6 puffs, 12 dc (US sc), 6 x 2ch sp, 12 x 3ch sp.

Round 5: (Col-1) join with ss in any corner sp, 5 ch (counts as first tr [US dc] and 2ch sp), tr (US dc) in same sp, tr (US dc) in next dc (US sc), 3 tr (US dc) in next 3ch sp, tr (US dc) in puff, 3 tr (US dc) in next 3ch sp, tr (US dc) in next dc (US sc), *(tr [US dc], 2 ch, tr [US dc]) in next corner sp, tr (US dc) in next dc (US sc), 3 tr (US dc) in next 3ch sp, tr (US dc) in puff, 3 tr (US dc) in next 3ch sp, tr (US dc) in next dc (US sc), repeat from * around, join with ss in 3rd ch of beginning ch, finish off — 66 tr (US dc).

Rounds 6, 7 and 8: See Finishing individual motifs, Joining new yarn A, and Continuing yarn B and C (Col-4).]]

MOTIF 12

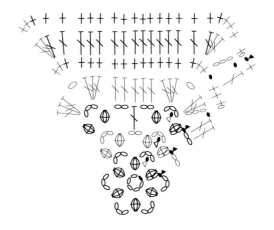 **Beginning cluster** uses 2 ch, 3 tr (US dc); 4 loops on hook.

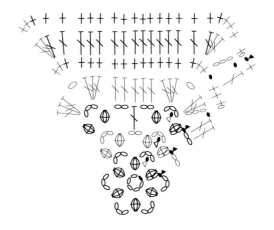 **Cluster** uses 4 tr (US dc); 5 loops on hook.

Assign Col-1, Col-2, Col-3 to the colours of your choice.

Begin with (Col-1) 5 ch, join with ss to form a ring.

Round 1: work beginning cluster, 3 ch, *cluster, 3 ch, repeat from * 5 times, join with ss in top of beginning cluster, finish off — 6 clusters, 6 x 3ch sp.

Round 2: (Col-3) join with ss in any 3ch sp, (beginning cluster, 3 ch, cluster) in same sp, 2 ch, *(cluster, 3 ch, cluster) in each 3ch sp, 2 ch, repeat from * around, join with ss in top of beginning cluster, finish off — 12 clusters, 6 x 2ch sp, 6 x 3ch sp.

Round 3: (Col-2) join with ss in any corner sp, (beginning cluster, 3 ch, cluster) in same sp, 2 ch, 1 tr (US dc) into next 2ch sp, 2 ch, *(cluster, 3 ch, cluster) into corner sp, 2 ch, 1 tr (US dc) into next 2ch sp, 2 ch, repeat from * around, join with ss in top of beginning cluster, finish off — 12 clusters, 6 tr (US dc), 12 x 2ch sp, 6 x 3ch sp.

Round 4: (Col-4) join with ss in any corner sp, 3 ch, (2 tr [US dc], 1 ch, 3 tr [US dc]) in same sp, 2 tr (US dc) in next 2ch sp, tr (US dc) in next tr (US dc), 2 tr (US dc) in next 2ch sp, *(3 tr [US dc], 1 ch, 3 tr [US dc]) in next corner sp, 2 tr (US dc) in next 2ch sp, tr (US dc) in next tr (US dc), 2 tr (US dc) in next 2ch sp, repeat from * around, join with ss to top of beginning ch, do not finish off — 66 tr (US dc).

Rounds 5, 6 and 7: See Finishing individual motifs, Continuing yarn A, B and C (Col-4).

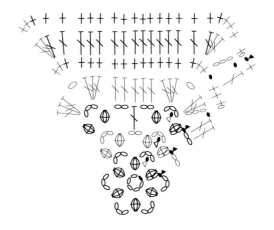

MOTIF 13

Beginning cluster uses 2 ch, 3 tr (US dc) — 4 loops on hook.

Cluster uses 4 tr (US dc) — 5 loops on hook.

Work quadruple treble/qtr (US triple treble/trtr) around foundation ring of Round 1, between clusters.

Work in back loops.

Assign Col-1, Col-2, Col-3 to the colours of your choice.

Begin with (Col-4) 5 ch, join with ss to form a ring.

Round 1: work beginning cluster, 3 ch, *cluster, 3 ch, repeat from * 5 times, join with ss in top of beginning cluster, finish off — 6 clusters, 6 x 3ch sp.

Round 2: (Col-1) join with ss in any 3ch sp, (2 ch, 2 htr [US hdc], 3 ch, 3 htr [US hdc]) in same sp, 1 ch, *(3 htr [US hdc], 3 ch, 3 htr [US hdc], 1 ch) in next 3ch sp, repeat from * around, join with ss to beginning ch, finish off — 12 htr (US hdc), 6 x 3ch sp, 6 x 1ch sp.

Round 3: (Col-3) join with ss in any 3ch sp, (3 ch, 1 tr [US dc], qtr [US trtr], 2 tr [US dc]) in same sp, dc (US sc) in next 3 htr (US hdc), dc (US sc) in next 1ch sp, dc (US sc) in next 3 htr (US hdc), *(2 tr [US dc], qtr [US trtr], 2 tr [US dc]) in next corner sp, dc (US sc) in next 3 htr (US hdc), dc (US sc) in next 1ch sp, dc (US sc) in next 3 htr (US hdc), repeat from * around, join with ss to beginning ch, finish off — 24 tr (US dc), 6 qtr (US trtr), 42 dc (US sc).

Round 4: (Col-2) (work in back loops only) join with ss in back loop of any qtr (US trtr), 3 ch, 2 tr (US dc) in same sp, dc (US sc) in next 11 sts, *3 tr (US dc) in corner st, dc (US sc) in next 11 sts, repeat from * around, join with ss in both loops of beginning ch, finish off — 18 tr (US dc), 66 dc (US sc), 84 sts total.

Round 5: (Col-4) (work in both loops) join with ss in any corner st, 3 ch, 2 tr (US dc) in same st, tr (US dc) in next tr (US dc), dtr in next 11 dc (US sc), tr (US dc) in next tr (US dc), *3 tr (US dc) in next corner st, tr (US dc) in next tr (US dc), dtr in next 11 dc (US sc), tr (US dc) in next tr (US dc), repeat from * around, join with ss to beginning ch, do not finish off — 30 tr (US dc), 66 dtr, 96 sts total.

Round 6: See Finishing individual motifs, Continuing yarn C (Col-4).

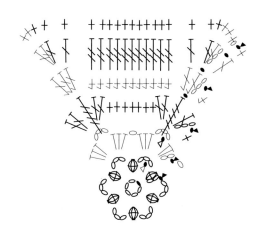

MOTIF 14

⊕ **Beginning cluster** uses 2 ch, 2 tr (US dc).

⊕ **Cluster** uses 3 tr (US dc).

⊕ **Beginning popcorn** uses 3 ch, 3 tr (US dc).

⊕ **Popcorn** uses 4 tr (US dc).

Assign Col-1, Col-2, Col-3, Col-4 to the colours of your choice.

Begin with (Col-4) 2 ch.

Round 1: (Col-4) 6 dc (US sc) in 2nd ch from hook, join with ss to first dc (US sc), finish off.

Round 2: (Col-3) join with ss in any dc (US sc), work beginning popcorn in same dc (US sc), 3 ch, *popcorn in next dc (US sc), 3 ch, repeat from * 5 times, join with ss to beginning popcorn, finish off — 6 popcorns, 6 x 3ch sp.

Round 3: (Col-2) join with ss in any 3ch sp, (work beginning cluster, 3 ch, cluster) in same sp, 1 ch, *(cluster, 3 ch, cluster) in next 3ch sp, 1 ch, repeat from * around, join with ss to beginning cluster, finish off — 12 clusters, 6 x 1ch sp.

Round 4: (Col-3) join with ss in any 3ch sp, (work beginning cluster, 3 ch, cluster) in same sp, 2 ch, cluster in next 1ch sp, 2 ch, *(cluster, 3 ch, cluster) in next 3ch sp, 2 ch, cluster in next 1ch sp, 2 ch, repeat from * around, join with ss to beginning cluster, finish off — 18 clusters, 12 x 2ch sp.

Round 5: (Col-1) join with ss in any 3ch sp, (2 ch, 2 htr [US hdc], 2 ch, 3 htr [US hdc], 2 ch) in same sp, (htr [US hdc] in next 2ch sp, 2 ch) twice, *(3 htr [US hdc], 2 ch, 3 htr [US hdc]) in next 3ch sp, 2 ch, (htr [US hdc] in next 2ch sp, 2 ch) twice, 2 ch, repeat from * around, join with ss to beginning ch, finish off — 48 htr (US hdc).

Round 6: (Col-4) join with ss in any corner sp, (3 ch, 2 tr [US dc]) in same sp, tr (US dc) in next 3 htr (US hdc), 2 tr (US dc) in next 2ch sp, 3 tr (US dc) in next 2ch sp, 2 tr (US dc) in next 2ch sp, tr (US dc) in next 3 htr (US hdc), *3 tr (US dc) in corner sp, tr (US dc) in next 3 htr (US hdc), 2 tr (US dc) in next 2ch sp, 3 tr (US dc) in next 2ch sp, 2 tr (US dc) in next 2ch sp, tr (US dc) in next 3 htr (US hdc), repeat from * around to last 3 htr

(US hdc), tr (US dc) in each of last 3 htr (US hdc), join with ss to beginning ch, finish off — 96 tr (US dc).

Round 7: See Finishing individual motifs, Continuing yarn C (Col-4).

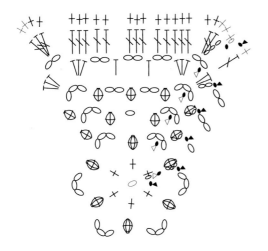

MOTIF 15

Assign Col-1, Col-2, Col-3 to the colours of your choice.

Begin with (Col-1) 3 ch, join with ss to form a ring.

Round 1: 3 ch (counts as 1 dc [US sc] plus 2 ch), into ring work (dc [US sc], 2 ch) 5 times, join with ss to bottom of beginning ch, finish off — 6 x 2ch sp.

Round 2: (Col-3) join with dc (US sc) in any 2ch sp, work (4 htr [US hdc], dc [US sc], ss) in same sp, *then work (dc [US sc], 4 htr [US hdc], dc [US sc], ss) in next 2ch sp, repeat from * around, do not join — 6 petals.

Round 3: (note: work behind petals and in 2ch sp on Round 1) 1 ch, *skip first 3 sts of next petal, force a dc (US sc) before next htr (US hdc), 4 ch, repeat from * around, join with ss to first dc (US sc), finish off — 6 x 4ch sp.

Round 4: (Col-2) join with ss in any 4ch sp, (3 ch, 2 tr [US dc], 2 ch, 3 tr [US dc]) in same sp, 1 ch, *(3 tr [US dc], 2 ch, 3 tr [US dc]), 1 ch, repeat from * around, join with ss to beginning ch, finish off — 36 tr (US dc), 6 x 2ch sp, 6 x 1ch sp.

Round 5: (Col-4) join with ss in any 2ch sp, 3 ch, (2 tr [US dc], 2 ch, 3 tr [US dc]) in same sp, 2 ch, tr (US dc) in next 1ch sp, 2 ch, * 3 tr (US dc), 2 ch, 3 tr (US dc) in corner sp, 2 ch, tr (US dc) in next 1ch sp, 2 ch, repeat from * around, join with ss to beginning ch, do not finish off — 42 tr (US dc).

Round 6: 3 ch, tr (US dc) in next 2 tr (US dc), 3 tr (US dc) in corner sp, tr (US dc) in next 3 tr (US dc), 2 tr (US dc) in next 2ch sp, tr (US dc) in next tr (US dc), 2 tr (US dc) in next 2ch sp, tr (US dc) in next 3 tr (US dc), *3 tr (US dc) in corner sp, tr (US dc) in next 3 tr (US dc), 2 tr (US dc) in next 2ch sp, tr (US dc) in next tr (US dc), 2 tr (US dc) in next 2ch sp, tr (US dc) in next 3 tr (US dc), repeat from * around, join with ss in beginning ch, do not finish off — 84 tr (US dc).

Rounds 7 and 8: See Finishing individual motifs, Continuing yarn B and C (Col-4).

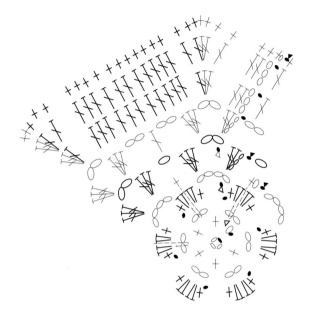

MOTIF 16

Slip stitch/ss from the back around the post of next tr (US dc).

Assign Col-1, Col-2, Col-3 to the colours of your choice.

Note: Work loosely when working flower.

Begin with (Col-3) 5 ch, join with ss to form a ring.

Round 1: (ss in ring, 3 tr [US dc] in ring) 6 times, join with ss to first ss, do not finish off — 6 petals.

Round 2: (work from behind petals; when joining with ss at end, skip 1 ch of beginning ch) 1 ch, skip next tr (US dc), ss from the back around the post of next tr (US dc), 3 ch, *skip next 2 tr (US dc), ss from the back around the post of next tr (US dc), 3 ch, repeat from * around, join with ss in first ss, finish off — 6 x 3ch sp.

Round 3: (Col-1) (ss, 5 tr [US dc], ss) in each 3ch sp around, join with ss in first ss, do not finish off — 6 petals.

Round 4: (when joining with ss at end, skip 2 ch of beginning ch) 2 ch, skip next 2 tr (US dc), ss from the back around the post of next tr (US dc), 4 ch, *skip next 4 tr (US dc), ss from the back around the post of next tr (US dc), 4 ch, repeat from * around, join with ss in first ss, finish off — 6 x 4ch sp.

Round 5: (Col-3) (ss, 7 tr [US dc], ss) in each 4ch sp around, join with ss in first ss, do not finish off — 6 petals.

Round 6: (when joining with ss at end, skip 3 ch of beginning ch) 3 ch, skip next 3 tr (US dc), ss from the back around the post of next tr (US dc),

5 ch, *skip next 6 tr (US dc), ss from the back around the post of next tr (US dc), 5 ch, repeat from * around, join with ss in first ss, finish off — 6 x 5ch sp.

Round 7: (Col-2) join with ss in ss behind any petal, 3 ch, 2 tr (US dc), 2 ch, 3 tr (US dc) in same sp, 3 ch, *(3 tr [US dc], 2 ch, 3 tr [US dc]) in next ss behind next petal, 3 ch, repeat from * around, join with ss to beginning ch, finish off — 36 tr (US dc), 6 x 2ch sp, 6 x 3ch sp.

Round 8: (Col-4) join with dc (US sc) in any 2ch sp, 2 dc (US sc) in same sp, *dc (US sc) in each tr (US dc), 3 dc (US sc) in each 3ch sp, 3 dc (US sc) in each corner sp, repeat from * around, join with ss to first dc (US sc), do not finish off — 66 dc (US sc).

Rounds 9, 10 and 11: See Finishing individual motifs, Continuing yarn A, B and C (Col-4).

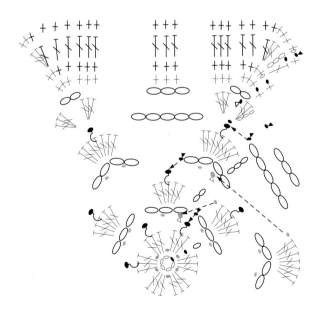

MOTIF 17

Long double crochet/Ldc (US Long single crochet/Lsc)

Long treble/Ltr (US Long double crochet/Ldc)

Assign Col-1, Col-2, Col-3, Col-4 to the colours of your choice.

Begin with (Col-4) 5 ch, join with ss to form a ring.

Round 1: 1 ch, 12 dc (US sc) in ring, join with ss to first dc (US sc), finish off.

Round 2: (Col-1) join with ss in any dc (US sc), 3 ch (counts as first tr [US dc], now and throughout), 2 tr (US dc) in same st, 1 ch, skip next dc (US sc), *3 tr (US dc) in next dc (US sc), 1 ch, skip next dc (US sc), repeat from * around; join with ss to beginning ch, finish off — 6 shells, 6 x 1ch sp.

Round 3: (note: Ldc [US Lsc] is worked around the next 1 ch and in the skipped dc [US sc] on Round 1) (Col-2) join with dc (US sc) in first tr (US dc) of any 3tr (US dc) group, 2 dc (US sc) in next tr (US dc), dc (US sc) in next tr (US dc), Ldc (US Lsc) in skipped dc (US sc) on Round 1, *dc (US sc) in next tr (US dc), 2 dc (US sc) in next tr (US dc), dc (US sc) in next tr (US dc), Ldc (US Lsc) in skipped dc (US sc) on Round 1, repeat from * around, join with ss to first dc (US sc), finish off.

Round 4: (note: work around sts on Round 3 and in tr [US dc] and 1ch sp on Round 2) (Col-3) join with ss in first tr (US dc) of any 3tr (US dc) group on Round 2, 3 ch, 2 Ltr (US Ldc) in next tr (US dc), Ltr (US Ldc) in next tr (US dc), work Ltr (US Ldc) in next 1ch sp before Ldc (US Lsc) and in same sp after Ldc (US Lsc), *Ltr (US Ldc) in next tr (US dc), 2 Ltr (US Ldc) in next tr (US dc), Ltr (US Ldc) in next tr (US dc), work Ltr (US Ldc) in next 1ch sp before Ldc (US Lsc) *and* in same sp after Ldc (US Lsc), repeat from * around, join with ss to beginning ch, finish off — 36 sts.

Round 5: (note: work dc [US sc] in back loops) (Col-4) join with dc (US sc) in back loop of last Ltr (US Ldc) made, dc (US sc) in next 2 sts, dc (US sc) in sp *before* next Ltr (US Ldc), dc (US sc) in next 3 Ltr (US Ldc), working *around* Round 4, work Ldc (US Lsc) on both loops of Ldc (US Lsc) on Round 3 below, *dc (US sc) in next 3 Ltr (US

Ldc) on Round 4, dc (US sc) in sp *before* next Ltr (US Ldc), dc (US sc) in next 3 Ltr (US Ldc), working around Round 4, work Ldc (US Lsc) on both loops of Ldc (US Lsc) on Round 3 below, repeat from * around, join with ss to first dc (US sc), do not finish off — 48 sts.

Round 6: (work in both loops) 3 ch, tr (US dc) in next 2 dc (US sc), (2 tr [US dc], 1 ch, 2 tr [US dc]) in next dc (US sc), *tr (US dc) in next 7 dc (US sc), (2 tr [US dc], 1 ch, 2 tr [US dc]) in next dc (US sc), repeat from * around, join with ss to first dc (US sc), do not finish off — 66 sts.

Rounds 7, 8 and 9: See Finishing individual motifs, Continuing yarn A, B and C (Col-4).

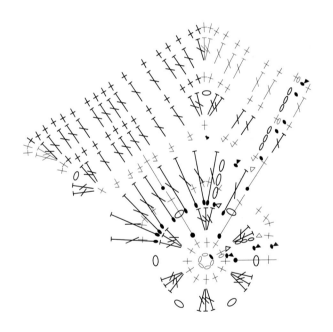

MOTIF 18

Long cluster/LC uses the 1ch sp on Round 2.

Assign Col-1, Col-2, Col-3 to the colours of your choice.

Begin with (Col-2) 4 ch, join with ss to form a ring.

Round 1: 3 ch (counts as first tr [US dc], now and throughout), work into ring (tr [US dc], 2 ch) once and then (2 tr [US dc], 2 ch) 5 times more, join with ss to beginning ch, finish off — 12 tr (US dc), 6 x 2ch sp.

Round 2: (Col-1) join with ss in any 2ch sp, 3 ch, tr (US dc), 2 ch, 2 tr (US dc) in same sp, 1 ch, *(2 tr [US dc], 2 ch, 2 tr [US dc]) in next 2ch sp, 1 ch, repeat from * around, join with ss to beginning ch, finish off — 24 tr (US dc), 6 x 2ch sp, 6 x 1ch sp.

Round 3: (Col-3) join with ss in any 2ch sp, 5 ch (counts as tr (US dc) plus 2 ch), tr (US dc) in

same sp, tr (US dc) in next 2 tr (US dc), 1 ch, tr (US dc) in next 2 tr (US dc), *(tr [US dc], 2 ch, tr [US dc]) in next 2ch sp, tr (US dc) in next 2 tr (US dc), 1 ch, tr (US dc) in next 2 tr (US dc), repeat from * around, join with ss to 3rd ch of beginning ch, finish off — 36 tr (US dc), 6 x 2ch sp, 6 x 1ch sp.

Round 4: (Col-2) join with dc (US sc) in any 2ch sp, 3 ch, dc (US sc) in same sp, dc (US sc) in next 3 tr (US dc), work LC, dc (US sc) in next 3 tr (US dc), *(dc [US sc], 3 ch, dc [US sc]) in next corner sp, dc (US sc) in next 3 tr (US dc), work LC, dc (US sc) in next 3 tr (US dc), repeat from * around, join with ss to first dc (US sc), finish off — 48 dc (US sc), 6 LC, 6 x 3ch sp.

Round 5: (Col-4) join with ss in any corner sp, 5 ch (counts as tr [US dc] plus 2 ch), tr (US dc) in same sp, tr (US dc) in each dc (US sc) and LC across to corner sp, *(tr [US dc], 2 ch, tr [US dc]) in corner sp, tr (US dc) in each dc (US sc) and LC across to corner sp, repeat from * around, join with ss to 3rd ch of beginning ch, do not finish off — 66 tr (US dc), 6 x 2ch sp.

Rounds 6, 7 and 8: See Finishing individual motifs, Continuing yarn A, B and C (Col-4).

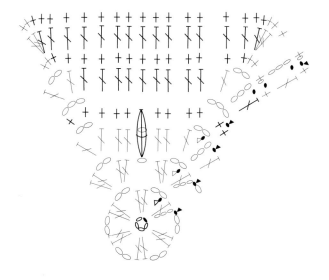

MOTIF 19

This pattern uses a 9-loop puff.

dc (US sc) decrease.

Assign Col-1, Col-2, Col-3 to the colours of your choice.

Begin with (Col-3) 5 ch, join with ss to form a ring.

Round 1: 1 ch, work puff, 3 ch, *puff, 3 ch, repeat from * 5 times, join with ss to first puff, finish off — 6 puffs, 6 x 3ch sp.

Round 2: (Col-2) join with ss in any 3ch sp, (1 ch, puff, 3 ch, puff) in same sp, 1 ch, *(puff, 3 ch, puff) in next 3ch sp, 1 ch, repeat from * around, join with ss in first puff, finish off — 12 puffs, 6 x 3ch sp, 6 x 1ch sp.

Round 3: (Col-1) join with dc (US sc) in any 3ch sp, 3 ch, dc (US sc) in same sp, 3 ch, dc (US sc) in next 1ch sp, 3 ch, *(dc [US sc], 3 ch, dc [US sc]) in next 3ch sp, 3 ch, dc (US sc) in next 1ch sp, 3 ch, repeat from * around, join with ss in first dc (US sc), do not finish off — 18 dc (US sc), 18 x 3ch sp.

Round 4: ss into corner sp, 1 ch, (dc [US sc], 3 ch, dc [US sc]) in same sp, dc (US sc) in next dc (US sc), 3 dc (US sc) in next 3ch sp, dc (US sc) in next dc (US sc), 3 dc (US sc) in next 3ch sp, dc (US sc) in next dc (US sc), *(dc [US sc], 3 ch, dc [US sc]) in corner sp, dc (US sc) in next dc (US sc), 3 dc (US sc) in next 3ch sp, dc (US sc) in next dc (US sc), 3 dc (US sc) in next 3ch sp, dc (US sc) in next dc (US sc), repeat from * around, join with ss in first dc (US sc), finish off — 66 dc (US sc), 6 x 3ch sp.

Round 5: From now on you will be working in rows, turning, decreasing and creating 6 triangles that radiate outward from your work. Alternate colours 2 and 3 and you will have 3 triangles of each colour.

5a. join with dc (US sc) (on left) of any 3ch sp, dc (US sc) in each dc (US sc) across, dc (US sc) in 3ch sp — 13 dc (US sc).

5b. 1 ch, turn, decrease next 2 dc (US sc), dc (US sc) in each dc (US sc) across to last 2 dc (US sc), decrease last 2 dc (US sc), continue in this way until 3 dc (US sc) remain.

5c. decrease first 2 dc (US sc), 2 ch, decrease 2nd and 3rd dc (US sc) (i.e. use 2nd dc [US sc] twice), finish off — 2 dc (US sc) at point.

Repeat a, b, and c for each side, alternating colours.

Round 6: When all triangles are complete you will be working between triangle corner tips, around, counting 15 dc (US sc) between the corner sts. (Col-4) join with dc (US sc) in first of the 2 dc (US sc) at top of point, 2 ch, *dc (US sc) in 2nd dc (US sc) of point, work 15 dc (US sc) evenly across to next point, dc (US sc) in first dc (US sc) of point, 2 ch, repeat from * around, join with ss to first dc (US sc), do not finish off — 90 dc (US sc), 6 x 2ch sp.

Round 7: 2 ch, *3 htr (US hdc) in next corner sp, htr (US hdc) in each dc (US sc) across, repeat from * around, join with ss to beginning ch, finish off — 108 htr (US hdc).

detail

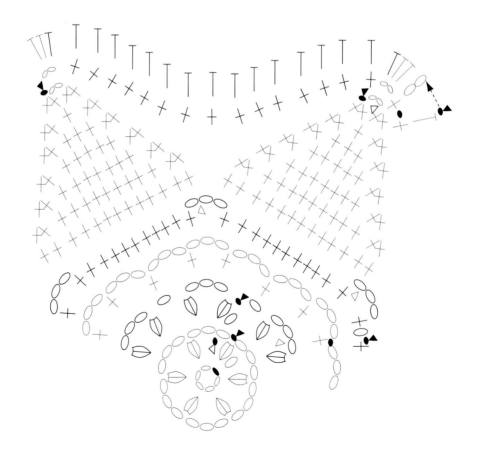

FINISHING

JOINING SQUARES

Lay out the 19 hexagons according to placement chart or as desired. Pin them together, working around the centre and out, taking care to always join the same way round. With right sides of hexagons facing outward, and joining only two at a time, work back loop of the hexagons being joined, using one of the joining methods listed under Techniques at the beginning of the book— invisible join (mattress stitch), visible or flat join (whip stitch), slip stitch join or dc (us sc) join. The dc (US sc) method, which is the strongest, was used for the sampler in the photo.

HEXAGON PLACEMENT CHART

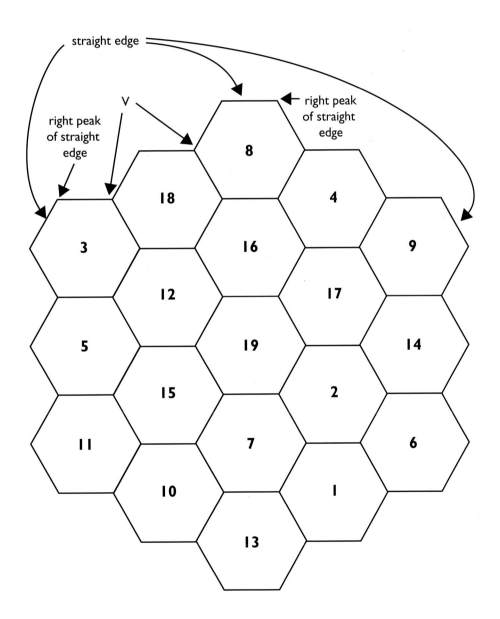

BORDER SURROUND

When all the hexagons have been joined together, the surround can be worked in Col-4.

Round 1: (for this round work in back loops only; and when working centre of V, work both joining loops as one dc [US sc] with right side facing) (Col-4) join with dc (US sc) in back loop of centre st of right peak of any straight edge, 2 dc (US sc) in same st, dc (US sc) in each st, 3 dc (US sc) in each peak around, join with ss to first dc (US sc), do not finish off.

Round 2: (from now work in both loops) 1 ch, dc (US sc) in same st, dc (US sc) in each dc (US sc) to corner, *(3 dc [US sc] in corner st, dc [US sc] in next 17 dc [US sc], skip next 3 dc [US sc], 3 ch, dc [US sc] in next 17 dc [US sc]) twice, 3 dc (US sc) in corner st, dc (US sc) in each dc (US sc) to next corner st, repeat from * around, join with ss to first dc (US sc), do not finish off.

Round 3: 1 ch, dc (US sc) in same st, dc (US sc) in each dc (US sc) to corner, *(3 dc [US sc] in corner st, dc [US sc] in next 15 dc [US sc], skip next 3 dc [US sc], 3 ch, dc [US sc] in next 3ch sp, 3 ch, skip next 3 dc [US sc], dc [US sc] in next 15 dc [US sc]) twice, 3 dc (US sc) in corner st, dc (US sc) in each dc (US sc) to next corner st, repeat from * around, join with ss to first dc (US sc), do not finish off.

Round 4: 1 ch, dc (US sc) in same st, dc (US sc) in each dc (US sc) to corner, *(3 dc [US sc] in corner st, dc [US sc] in next 13 dc [US sc], skip next 3 dc [US sc], 4 ch, {dc [US sc] in next 3ch sp, 4 ch, twice}, skip next 3 dc [US sc], dc [US sc] in next 13 dc [US sc]) twice, 3 dc (US sc) in corner st, dc (US sc) in each dc (US sc) to next corner st,

repeat from * around, join with ss to first dc (US sc), do not finish off.

Round 5: 1 ch, dc (US sc) in same st, dc (US sc) in each dc (US sc) to corner, *(3 dc [US sc] in corner st, dc [US sc] in next 11 dc [US sc], skip next 3 dc [US sc], 5 ch, {dc [US sc] in next 4ch sp, 5 ch, three times} skip next 3 dc [US sc], dc [US sc] in next 11 dc [US sc]) twice, 3 dc (US sc) in corner st, dc (US sc) in each dc (US sc) to next corner st, repeat from * around, join with ss to first dc (US sc), do not finish off.

Round 6: 1 ch, dc (US sc) in same st, dc (US sc) in each dc (US sc) to corner, *(3 dc [US sc] in corner st, dc [US sc] in next 9 dc [US sc], skip next 3 dc [US sc], 6 ch, {dc [US sc] in next 5ch sp, 6 ch, four times}, skip next 3 dc [US sc], dc [US sc] in next 9 dc [US sc]) twice, 3 dc (US sc) in corner st, dc (US sc) in each dc (US sc) to next corner st, repeat from * around, join with ss to first dc (US sc), do not finish off.

Round 7: 1 ch, dc (US sc) in same st, dc (US sc) in each dc (US sc) to corner, *(3 dc [US sc] in corner st, dc [US sc] in next 7 dc [US sc], skip next 3 dc [US sc], 6 ch, {dc [US sc] in next 6ch sp, 6 ch, five times}, skip next 3 dc [US sc], dc [US sc] in next 7 dc [US sc]) twice, 3 dc (US sc) in corner st, dc (US sc) in each dc (US sc) to next corner st, repeat from * around, join with ss to first dc (US sc), do not finish off.

Round 8: 1 ch, dc (US sc) in same st, dc (US sc) in each dc (US sc) to corner, *(3 dc [US sc] in corner st, dc [US sc] in next 5 dc [US sc], skip next 3 dc [US sc], 5 ch, {dc [US sc] in next 6ch sp, 5 ch, six times}, skip next 3 dc [US sc], dc [US sc] in next 5 dc [US sc]) twice, 3 dc (US sc) in corner st, dc (US sc) in each dc (US sc) to next corner st, repeat from * around, join with ss to first dc (US sc), do not finish off.

Round 9: 1 ch, dc (US sc) in same st, dc (US sc) in each dc (US sc) to corner, *(3 dc [US sc] in corner st, dc [US sc] in next 3 dc [US sc], skip next 3 dc [US sc], 4 ch, {dc [US sc] in next 5ch sp, 4 ch, seven times}, skip next 3 dc [US sc], dc [US sc] in next 3 dc [US sc]) twice, 3 dc (US sc) in corner st, dc (US sc) in each dc (US sc) to next corner st, repeat from * around, join with ss to first dc (US sc), do not finish off.

Round 10: 1 ch, dc (US sc) in same st, dc (US sc) in each dc (US sc), 3 dc (US sc) in each corner st, 4 dc (US sc) in each 4ch sp, around, join with ss to first dc (US sc), do not finish off.

Rounds 11, 12 and 13: (or see alternative) 1 ch, dc (US sc) in same st, dc (US sc) in each dc (US sc), 3 dc (US sc) in each corner st, around, join with ss to first dc (US sc), do not finish off

Round 14: 1 ch, ss in same st, **ss** in each dc (US sc) around, join with **ss** to first **ss**, finish off.

Alternative: Finish off Round 10 and bring in Cols 2, 3 and 4 for each following round.

Round 11: (Col-2) join with dc (US sc) in any corner st, 2 dc (US sc) in same st, dc (US sc) in each dc (US sc), 3 dc (US sc) in each corner st around, join with ss to first dc (US sc), finish off.

Round 12: (Col-3) join with dc (US sc) in any corner st, dc (US sc) in each dc (US sc) around, join with ss to first dc (US sc), finish off.

Round 13: (Col-4) join with dc (US sc) in any corner st, work crab st (*see below*) in each dc (US sc) around, join with ss to first dc (US sc), finish off.

Crab stitch: (reverse dc [US sc] always worked on right side and in the opposite direction to the usual) join where needed, 1 ch, *insert hook into the next st on right, YO and draw up a loop, YO and draw through both loops on hook, repeat from * around.

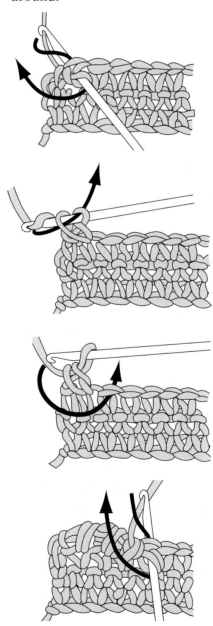

Corner clusters: (Col-4) This optional finishing touch is worked in all centre joins where hexagons meet.

One stitch cluster/OSC (uses one ch, st or sp as pattern indicates) with right side facing, join with ss in any joining st of hexagon, 3 ch, YO, insert hook in 3rd ch from hook, YO and pull up a loop, YO and draw through 2 loops on hook, (YO, insert hook in same ch, YO and pull up a loop, YO and draw through 2 loops on hook) twice more, YO and draw through all 4 loops on hook.

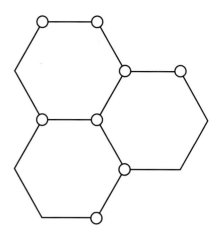

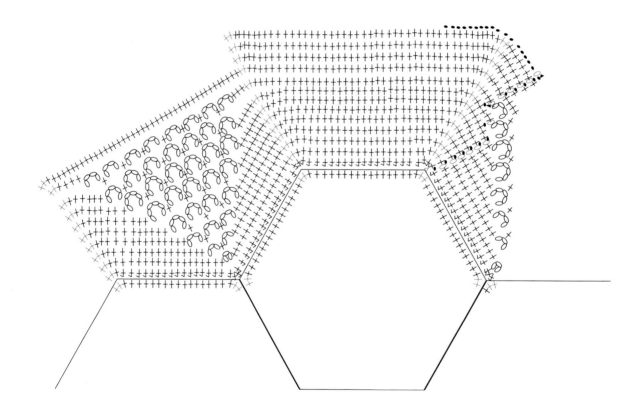

TASSELLED FRINGES

Plain fringe: wind yarn around a 5 cm (2 in) wide, or other desired size, piece of cardboard. Cut yarn along one edge. With wrong side facing, using ordinary crochet hook and two or more strands of yarn, fold yarn in half and draw loop through a stitch, draw ends through this loop and pull tightly to knot.

Fancy fringe: make a plain fringe, then, working over a 2.5 cm (1 in) wide, or other desired size, piece of cardboard, knot half the strands of yarn from adjoining sections together, as shown in the last diagram.

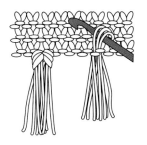 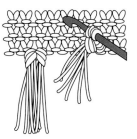 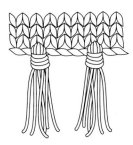 

wrong side   right side   fancy fringe

JACQUARD 30-MOTIF SAMPLER
LEVEL: AVERAGE TO ADVANCED

The ability to work double crochet (US single crochet) and the willingness to read a grid are all that's required for this colourful technique.

REQUIREMENTS For the rug in the photo I used a 4.40 (US G) crochet hook and approximately 550 g Panda Magnum 8-ply wool in Navy, together with an assortment of 8-ply yarn n various colours from my scrap basket. Jacquard is a great way of using up odds and ends.

CROCHET TECHNIQUE FOR ALL SQUARES

Foundation chain: make 32 ch.

Row 1: using the graph as guide, work dc (US sc) in the colour indicated in 2nd ch from hook and in each ch across — 31 dc (US sc).

Rows 2 to 31: using graph as guide, work dc (US sc) in colour indicated in each dc (US sc) across — 31 dc (US sc).

EDGING

Round 1: with right side facing and working from right to left, join with dc (US sc) in first dc (US sc) of last row, work 2 dc (US sc) in same st, then work 29 dc (US sc) evenly across each side with 3 dc (US sc) in each corner st around, join with ss to first dc (US sc), do not finish off — 128 dc (US sc).

Round 2: 1 ch, dc (US sc) in same st, work dc (US sc) in each dc (US sc) to next corner st, 3 dc (US sc) in each corner stitch around, join with ss in first dc (US sc), finish off — 136 dc (US sc).

MARKERS

Use markers to identify right side of work and corner stitches in edging.

GRAPH PAPER

Graph paper is ideal for working out patters, stitch placement and designs if you wish to create your own.

WORKING WITH THE COLOUR GRID

In jacquard a chart, graph or grid is used instead of written instructions for coloured patterns. Each square equals a stitch, each line equals a row. Each coloured square equals a secondary colour and each **blank square** equals the **main colour**.

Follow grids from the *bottom*. Read right-side rows from right to left, and wrong-side rows from left to right. You will find a steel ruler helpful to highlight the working row.

For those of you who enjoy working in this technique, look out for other needlework charts, such as cross-stitch patterns, which can be worked in this manner. You will be pleasantly surprised at what can be done with simple double crochet (US single crochet).

CHANGING COLOUR AND JOINING IN YARN

There are two methods of changing colour; using floats (which involves weaving cut ends into the back of the work) and working over colours not in use, which gives a reversible finish.

FLOATS

Floats are the lengths of yarn picked up and dropped mid-row, then cut, to make the pattern.

When 2 loops of last st colour remain on hook, drop old colour, pick up new colour and draw through 2 loops to complete st in new colour. Remember to leave long ends to weave in later.

The more floats you use the more weaving in there will be.

WORKING OVER COLOURS NOT IN USE

Carry unused colour of previous row along as you work in the new colour, picking up the stitch and unused yarn together.

This method uses more yarn but gives you a reversible finish.

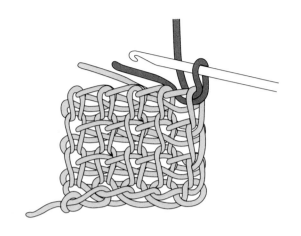

CHANGING COLOUR

When 2 loops of last st colour remain on hook, drop old colour, pick up new colour and draw through 2 loops to complete st.

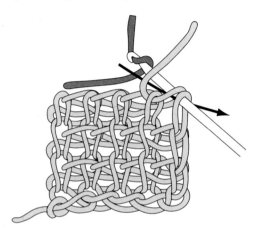

SQUARE 1: CHECKS

Using graph as guide, carry and work over each colour alternately.

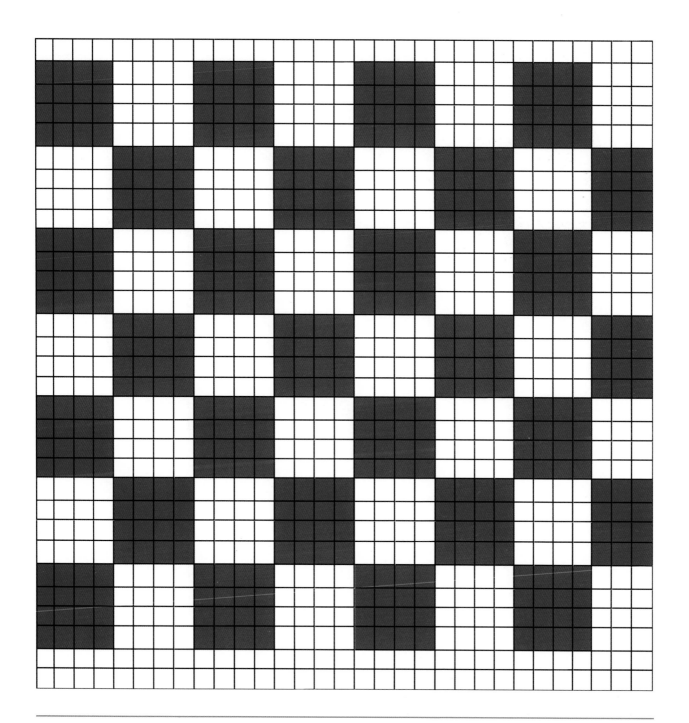

main colour   2nd colour

SQUARE 2: TRI-CHECKS

Using graph as guide, carry and work over each colour alternately.

☐ main colour   ▨ 2nd colour

SQUARE 3: BOX CHECKS

Using graph as guide, work coloured boxes as floats.

Carry and work over main colour through boxes.

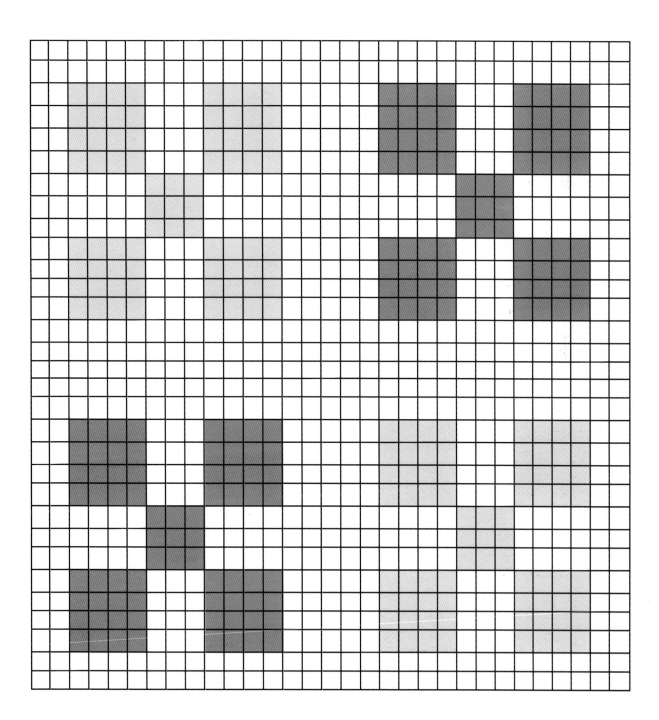

main colour   2nd colour   3rd colour

SQUARE 4: DIAMOND CHECK

Using graph as guide, carry and work over each colour alternately.

main colour   2nd colour

SQUARE 5: STAGGERED TRIANGLES

Using graph as guide, carry and work over each colour alternately.

main colour   2nd colour   3rd colour

SQUARE 6: SQUARES

Using graph as guide, work coloured squares as floats.

Carry and work over main colour through squares.

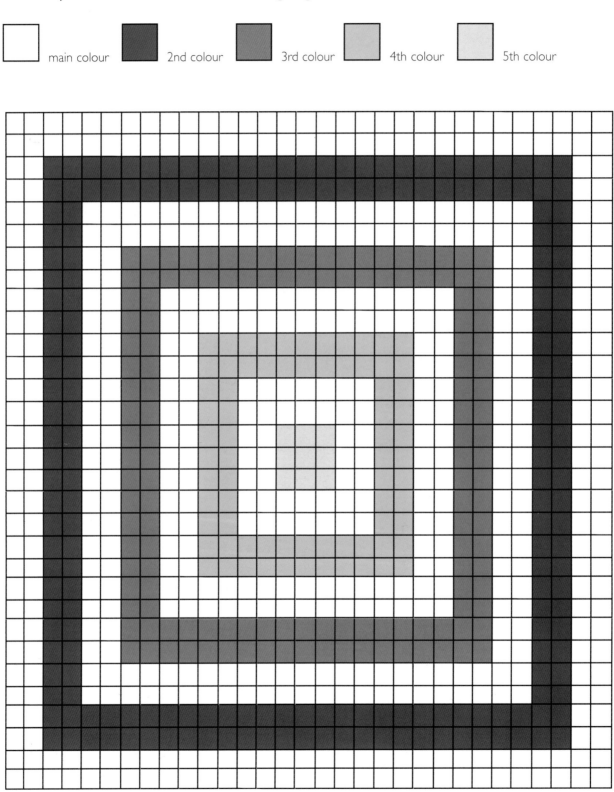

main colour   2nd colour   3rd colour   4th colour   5th colour

SQUARE 7: WINDMILLS

Using graph as guide, carry and work over each colour alternately.

□ main colour   ■ 2nd colour

SQUARE 8: STRAIGHTS

Using graph as guide, carry and work over each colour alternately.

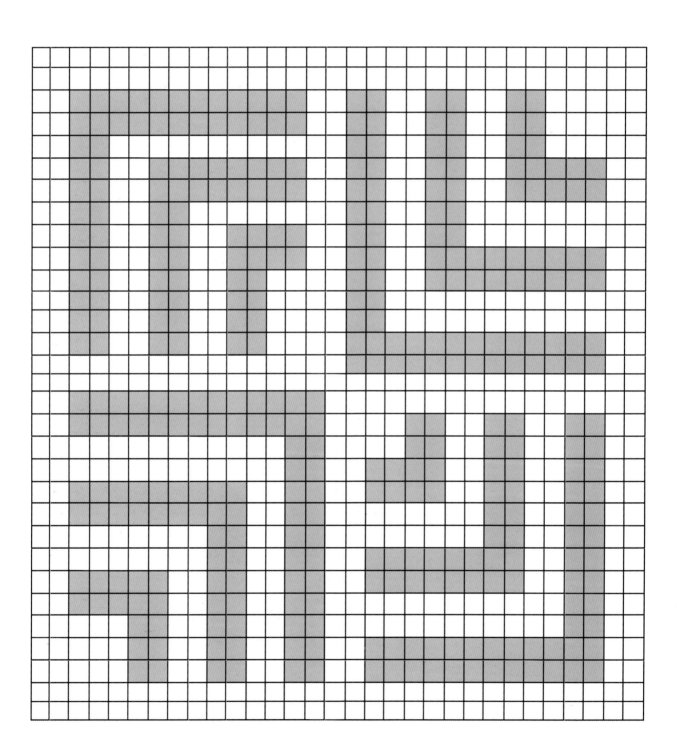

main colour   2nd colour

SQUARE 9: RIGHT ANGLES

Using graph as guide, work coloured right angles as floats.

Carry and work over main colour through boxes.

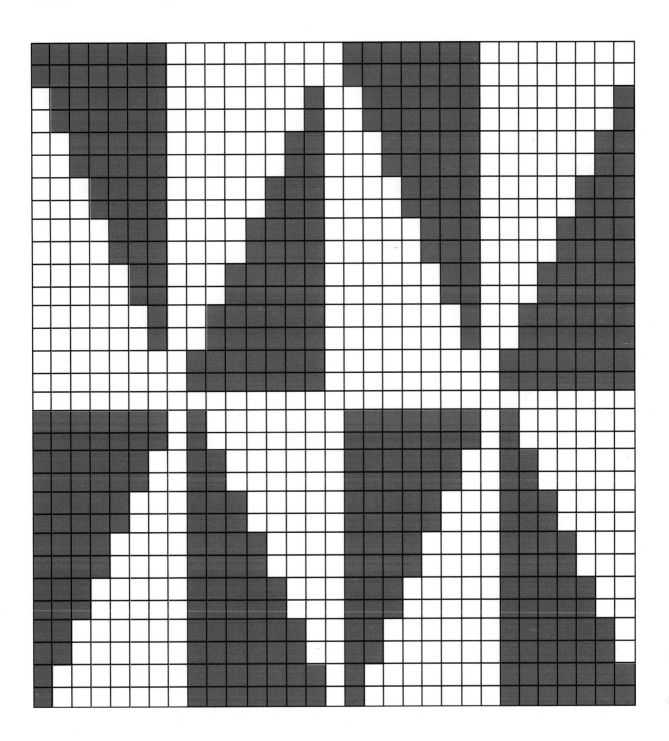

main colour   2nd colour

SQUARE 10: CROSSES

Using graph as guide, work coloured crosses as floats.

Carry and work over main colour through crosses.

☐ main colour   ▨ 2nd colour

SQUARE 11: BOX IN DIAMOND

Using graph as guide, work diamond and box as floats.

    Carry and work over main colour through diamond and box.

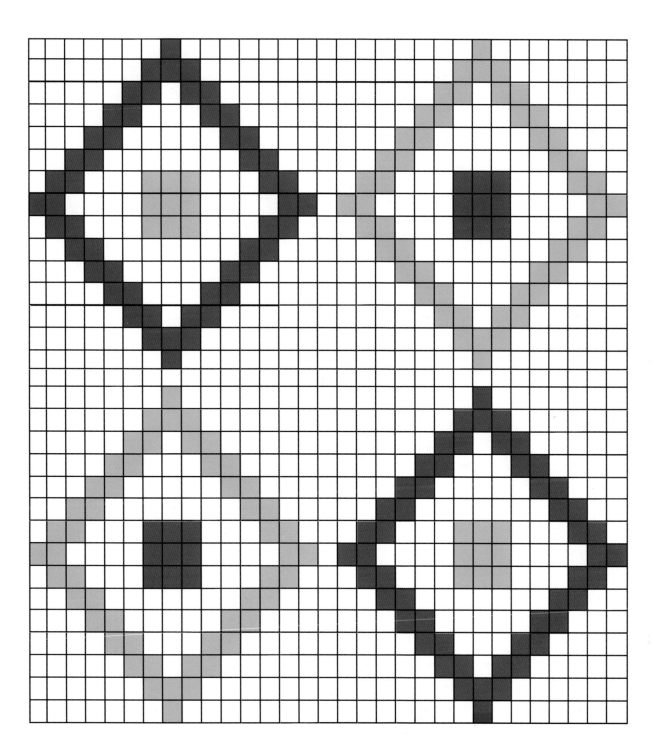

main colour   2nd colour   3rd colour

SQUARE 12: DOUBLE DIAMONDS

Using graph as guide, carry and work over each colour alternately.

□ main colour   □ 2nd colour

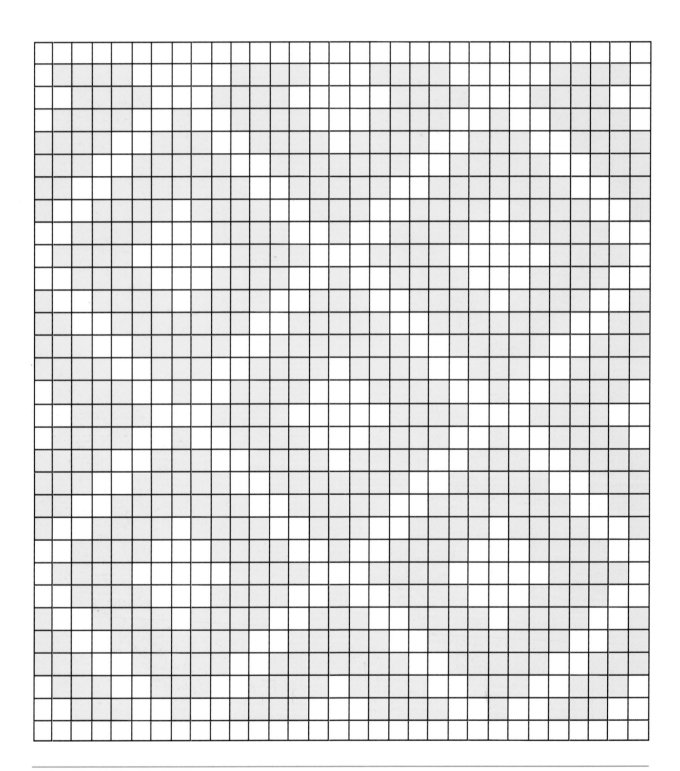

SQUARE 13: DIAMONDS

Using graph as guide, work coloured diamonds as floats.

Carry and work over main colour through diamonds.

main colour   2nd colour   3rd colour

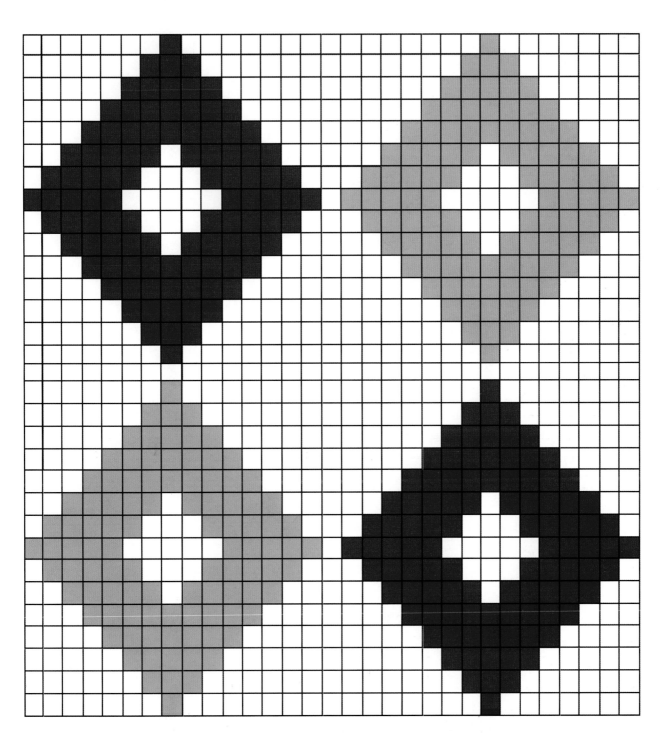

SQUARE 14: CHEQUERBOARD 1

Using graph as guide, work diamond checks as floats.

Carry and work over main colour through diamond checks.

☐ main colour   ■ 2nd colour

SQUARE 15: CHEQUERBOARD 2

Using graph as guide, carry and work over each colour alternately.

main colour 2nd colour

SQUARE 16: THREE-COLOUR DIAMONDS

Using graph as guide, work coloured diamonds as floats.

Carry and work over main colour through diamonds.

main colour   2nd colour   3rd colour   4th colour

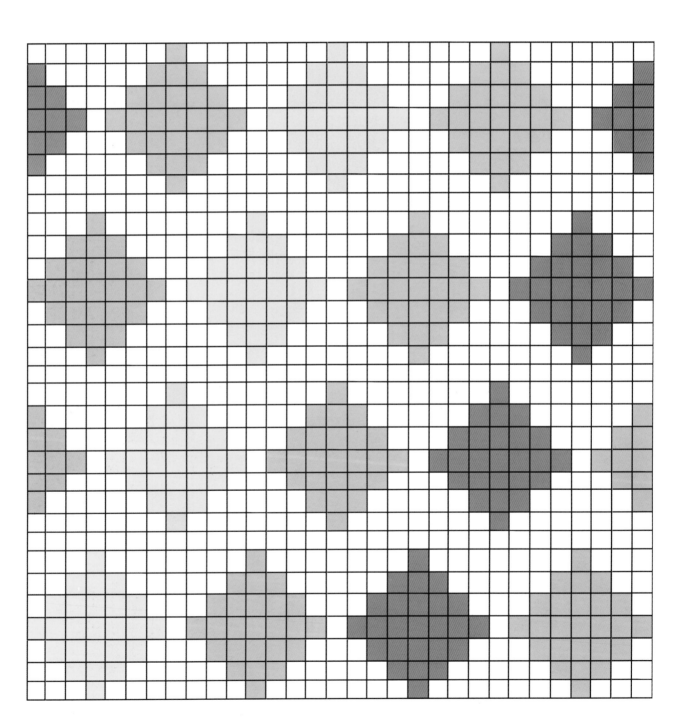

SQUARE 17: DIAMOND HARMONY

Using graph as guide, work each row of diamonds as floats, carrying and working over each colour alternately.

main colour   2nd colour   3rd colour

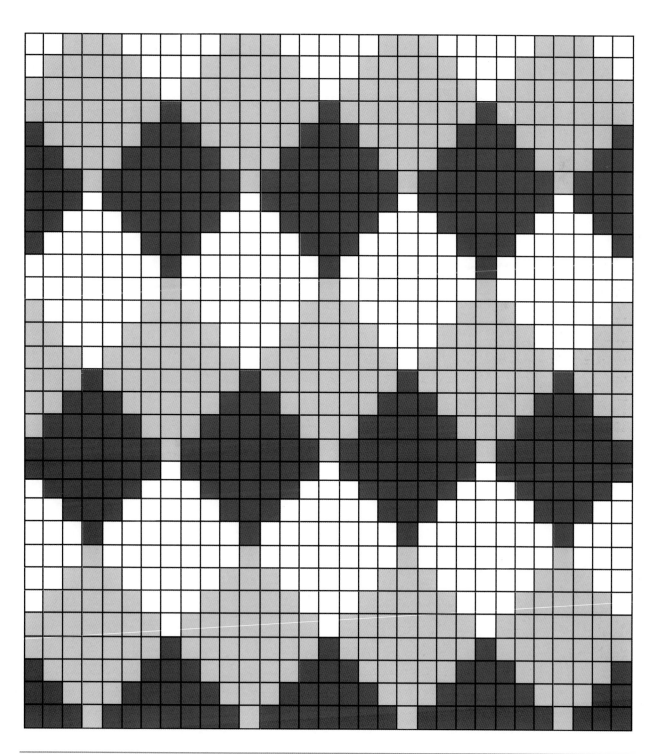

SQUARE 18: SNOWFLAKE 1

Using graph as guide, work snowflakes as floats.

Carry and work over main colour through snowflakes.

□ main colour   ▨ 2nd colour

SQUARE 19: SNOWFLAKE 2

Using graph as guide, work snowflakes as floats.

Carry and work over main colour through snowflakes.

☐ main colour   ■ 2nd colour

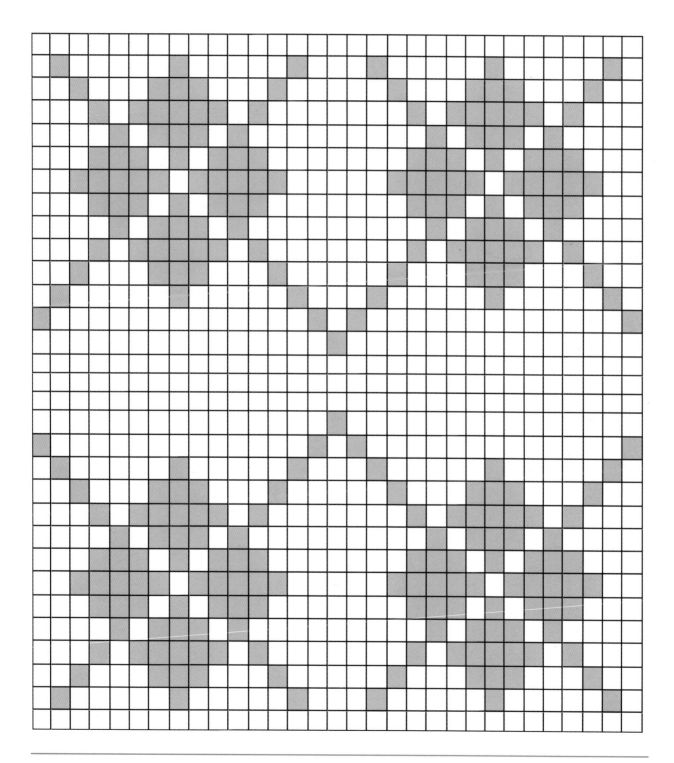

SQUARE 20: TARGET

Using graph as guide, work coloured circles as floats.

Carry and work over main colour through circles.

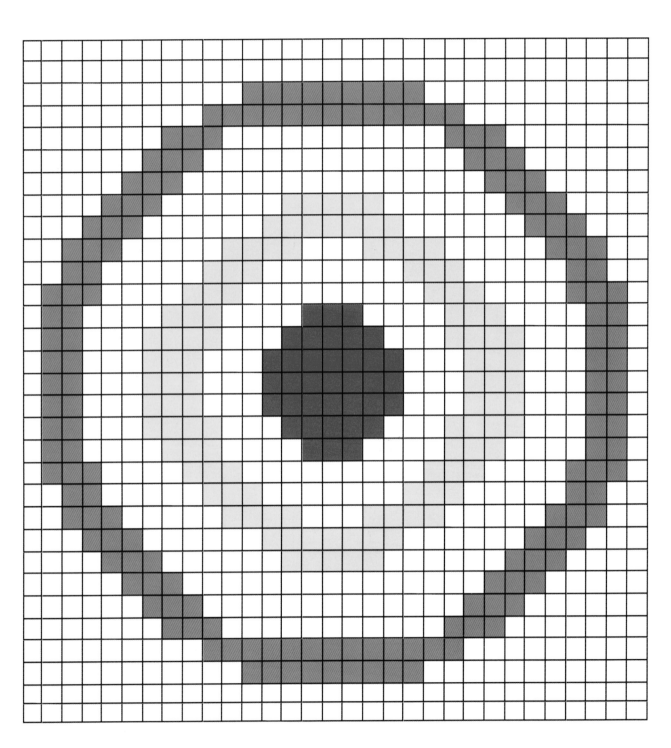

□ main colour   ▨ 2nd colour   ▢ 3rd colour   ■ 4th colour

SQUARE 21: SHORT STAGGERED CHEVRONS

Using graph as guide, work chevrons as floats.

Carry and work over main colour through chevrons.

☐ main colour ■ 2nd colour

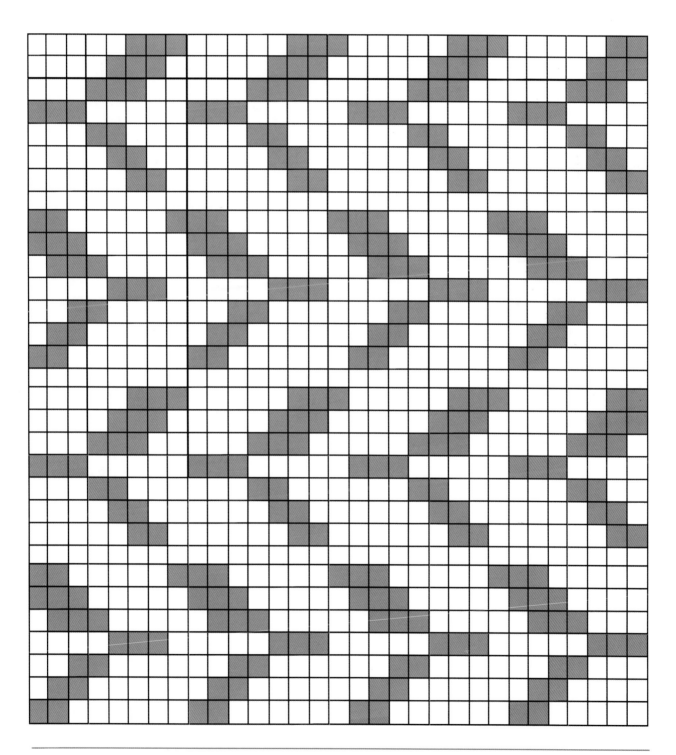

SQUARE 22: LONG STAGGERED CHEVRONS

Using graph as guide, work chevrons as floats.

Carry and work over main colour through chevrons.

☐ main colour ▨ 2nd colour

SQUARE 23: CHEVRON I

Using graph as guide, work chevrons as floats.

 Carry and work over main colour through chevrons.

□ main colour   ▨ 2nd colour   ■ 3rd colour

SQUARE 24: CHEVRON 2

Using graph as guide, work chevrons as floats.

Carry and work over main colour through chevrons.

main colour   2nd colour   3rd colour

SQUARE 25: DIAMONDS, MINI CHEVRONS AND STRIPES

Using graph as guide, work diamonds and chevrons as floats as indicated.

Carry and work over main colour through diamonds and chevrons as indicated.

Join stripe where indicated, carrying and working over main colour.

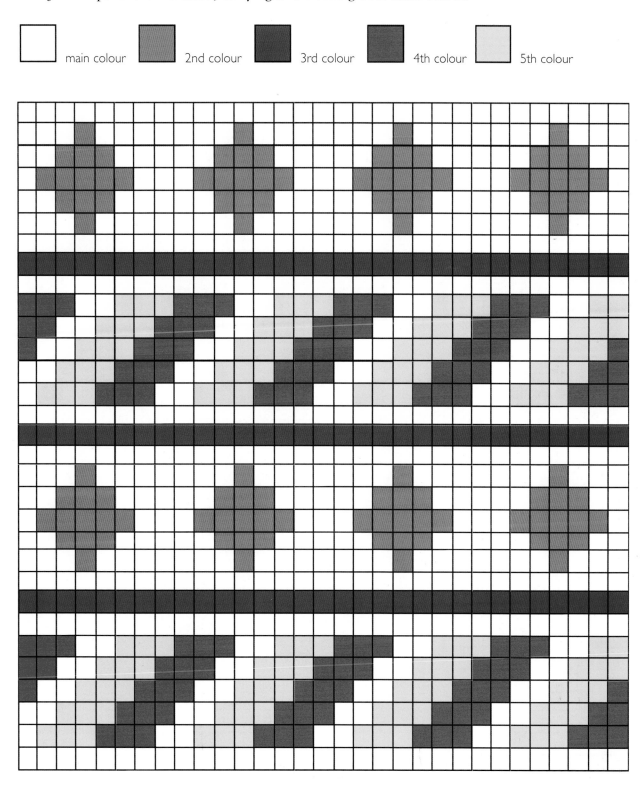

main colour   2nd colour   3rd colour   4th colour   5th colour

SQUARE 26: CHEQUERBOARD 3

Using graph as guide, carry and work over each colour and motif alternately.

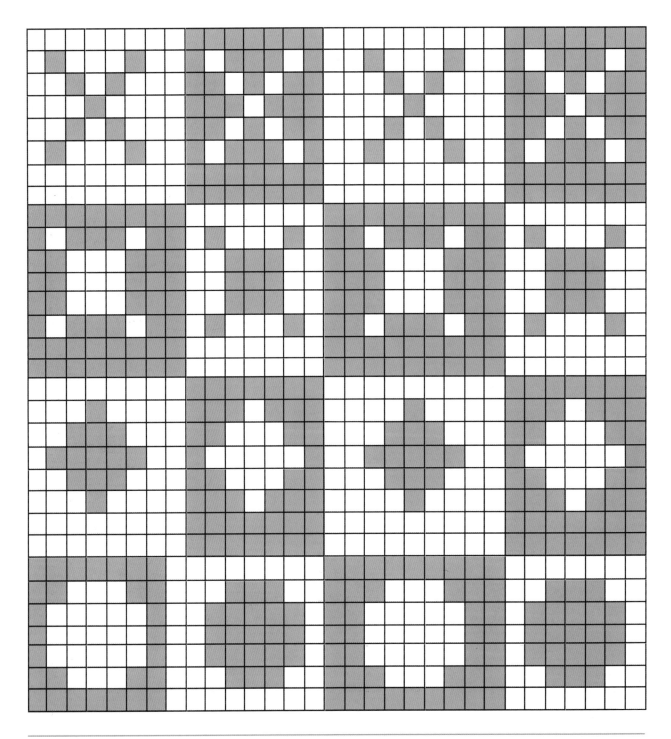

☐ main colour ▨ 2nd colour

SQUARE 27: HEARTS AND CROSSES

Using graph as guide, work coloured hearts, cross and box as floats.

Carry and work over main colour through hearts, cross and box.

main colour   2nd colour   3rd colour   4th colour

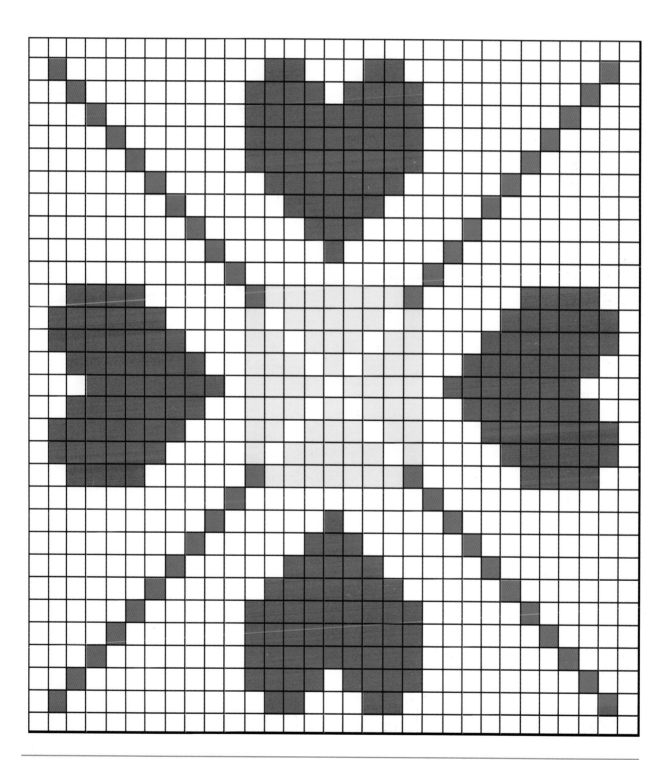

SQUARE 28: FRAMED BOXES

Using graph as guide, carry and work over each colour alternately.

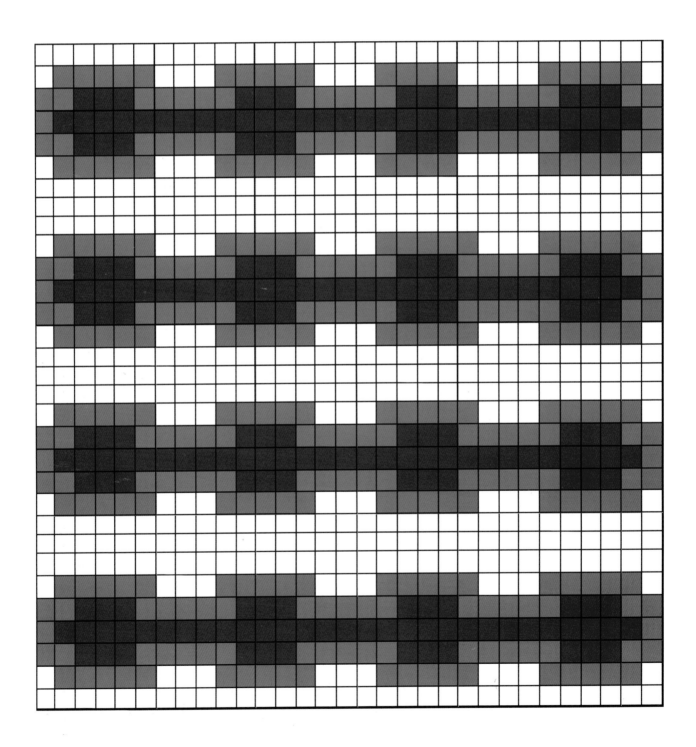

□ main colour   ▨ 2nd colour   ■ 3rd colour

SQUARE 29: TARTAN

Using graph as guide, carry and work over each colour alternately.

□ main colour ■ 2nd colour ▢ 3rd colour

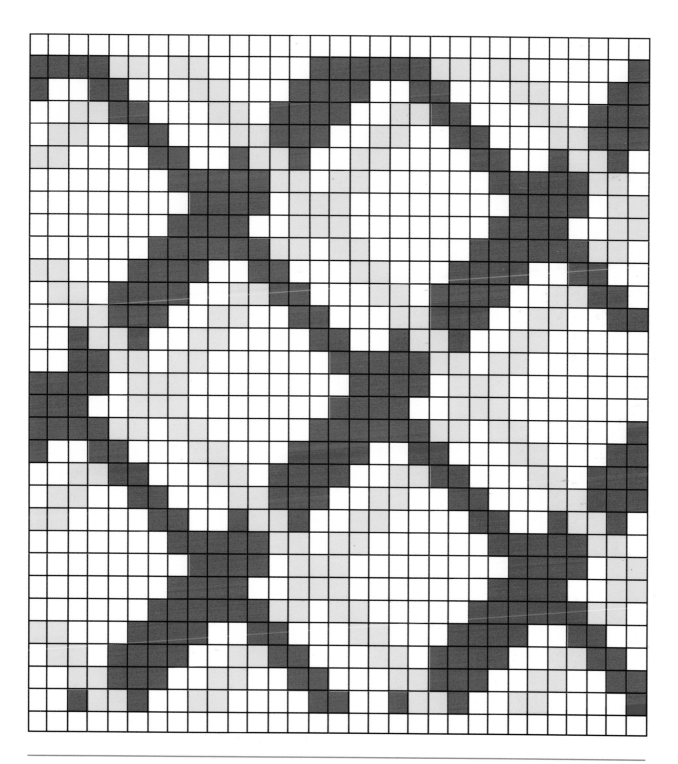

SQUARE 30: 3-D DIAMOND

Using graph as guide, work coloured sections of diamonds as floats.

Carry and work over main colour through each colour section.

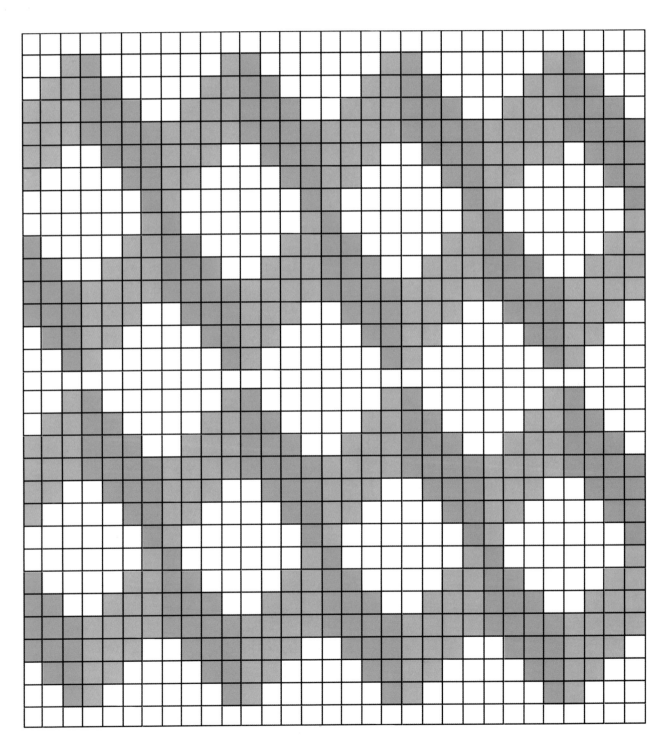

JOINING SQUARES

Lay out squares according to placement chart or as desired.

Pin the squares together, for easier handling working with 2 rows of squares at a time. Take care to always join from the same end for each row being joined.

Working from right to left, with right sides of both squares facing outward, work back loop (centre loops) of both squares, join in first sts using one of the joining methods listed under Techniques at the beginning of the book—invisible join (mattress stitch), slip stitch join or dc (us sc) join. The dc (US sc) method, which is the strongest, was used for the sampler in the photo.

7 Windmill	23 Chevron 1	4 Diamond check	21 Short staggered chevrons	8 Straights
24 Diamond, mini-chevrons & stripes	19 Snowflake 2	9 Right angles	1 Checks	16 Three-colour diamond
17 Diamond harmony	20 Target	28 Framed boxes	5 Staggered triangles	13 Diamonds
27 Hearts & crosses	11 Box in diamond	18 Snowflake 1	15 Chequer- board 2	3 Box checks
10 Crosses	29 Tartan	26 Chequer- board 3	6 Squares	14 Chequer- board 1
24 Chevron 2	2 Tri-checks	4 Double diamonds	30 3-D diamond	22 Long staggered chevrons

ALL-ROUND BORDER

Round 1: (work in Main Col and both loops) when all squares are joined, join Main Col with dc (US sc) in any corner st, 2 dc (US sc) in same st, *dc in each st across to next corner st, 3 dc (US sc) in corner st, repeat from * around, join with ss to first dc dc (US sc), do not finish off.

Round 2: (for picot st see below) continuing with Main Col, 1 ch, dc (US sc) in same st, (dc [US sc], picot st, dc [US sc]) in next corner st, *work 3 dc (US sc), 1 picot st, 3 dc (US sc) across to next corner st, (dc [US sc], 1 picot st, dc [US sc]) in corner st, repeat from * around, join with ss to first dc (US sc), finish off.

Picot stitch: Make 1 dc (US sc) in next st, 3 ch, then ss in 3rd ch from hook (picot made).

TUNISIAN SAMPLER RUG
LEVEL: ABOVE AVERAGE TO ADVANCED

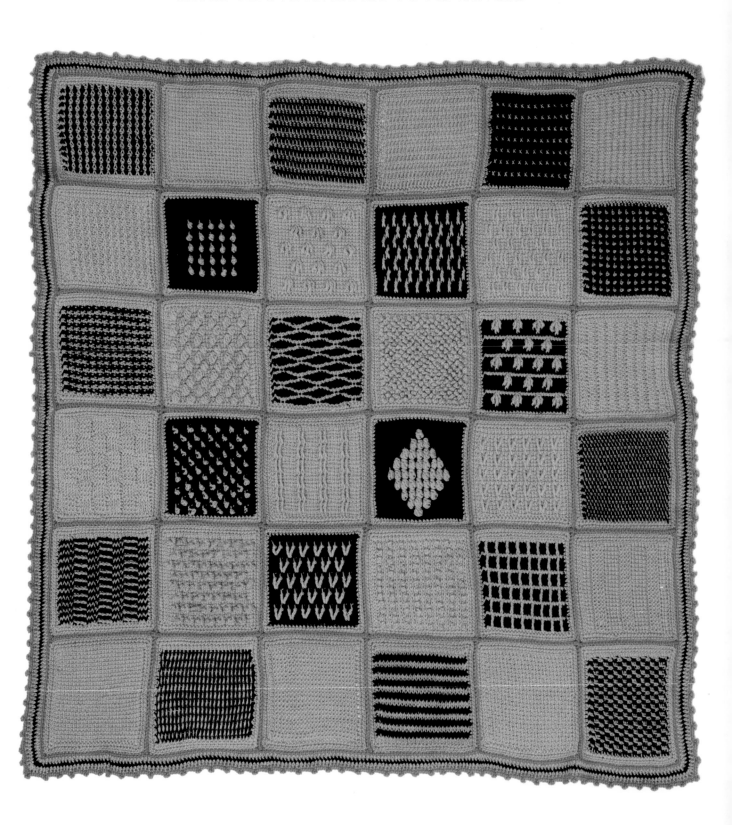

REQUIREMENTS For the rug in the photo I used a 4.50 (US G) Tunisian crochet hook for the main squares and a 4.00 (US F) ordinary hook for foundation chain, last row and edging. I used approximately 600 g Lincraft Double Knitting 8-ply wool in Ochre (Col-A) and 200 g Lincraft Double Knitting 8-ply wool in Chocolate (Col-B) for the main squares, and 100 g Lincraft Cosy Wool 8-ply in Orange (Col-C) for the edges and main border.

Somewhere between crochet and knitting, Tunisian crochet (also known as tricot) is worked on a long hook, not unlike a knitting needle, and produces a rich-textured, woven fabric.

In the past Tunisian crochet or tricot (pronounced *tree-coe*) crochet, roughly translated as 'French knitting', has been known by a variety of names—shepherd's crochet, Scottish (*écossais*) crochet, Russian crochet, fool's crochet and railway knitting. More recently it has been known as tricoter and Tunisian crochet, and in America as Afghan crochet. The fabric produced by this crochet method has a thick, firm, woven appearance and uses more yarn per row than either crochet or knitting.

This form of crochet is worked on a long hook and incorporates 2 basic rows—a pick-up row and a cast-off row—which are classed as one row. In many patterns these basic rows may be referred to as a 'row of simple stitch' or a 'row of basic tricot'. (Older patterns may refer to them as the *outward* and *return* rows, rows *1 and 2* or parts *A and B* of one row.)

The work is never turned (unless otherwise stated in the pattern) so the right side is always facing as you work.

For the best result, use a regular crochet hook one or two sizes smaller than the Tunisian crochet hook for the foundation chain, last row and edgings.

Because there are so many variations within each stitch, each giving a unique effect (for example, colour change from left to right or right to left/2 sts in one colour/4 sts in the next and so on), it's a good idea to make swatches using 16 or so foundation ch and trying out the combinations before starting your project.

Graph paper is ideal for working out patterns, stitch placement and designs.

COMMON TRICOT PROBLEMS AND TIPS FOR SOLVING THEM

WORK CURLING

This happens because the work isn't being turned. The edging, which is added later, will counteract this. Blocking is also helpful here.

You can also try threading a knitting needle through the 1st or 2nd row to add some weight to your work when some length has been gained.

LEFT-HAND EDGE LOOKS UNTIDY

Insert hook through both the last vertical bar and the vertical strand directly behind it.

When changing colour, keep a firm hold on the loops where the yarn is being dropped and picked up.

RIGHT HAND SIDE IS LOOSE AND SLOPPY

Keep yarn firm (but not tight) when making the 1st pick-up stitch.

WORK LEANING TO THE RIGHT

Make sure you are going into the 2nd vertical bar, not the first, and that you are picking up the *front* vertical bar.

LOSING OR GAINING STITCHES ON ROWS

Make sure you are picking up the *last* vertical bar, *and* that you are picking up the vertical bars, not the horizontal bars.

WORK LACKS HEIGHT

When picking up loops, the *hook should sit on top of work*. The hook sitting in front of the work both shortens the length of the stitch and uses more yarn than necessary.

BASIC TRICOT/BT

One complete row is equal to:

◉ 1 pick-up row (you should have the same number of loops on hook as foundation ch) plus

◉ 1 cast-off row (you should be left with one loop on hook).

Foundation chain Use an ordinary crochet hook 1 or 2 sizes *smaller* than tricot hook and make the number of chains required for length.

Last row Use an ordinary crochet hook 1 or 2 sizes *smaller* than tricot hook (the same size hook used for foundation chain) and continue working in the vertical bars in either dc (US sc) or ss (1 ch, dc [US sc]/ss) in very first bar and then in each bar across; finish off.

EDGING THE SQUARES

Use ordinary crochet hook the same size as foundation chain and last row.

As you work each square according to the instructions, finish it with these two rounds of edging. If you don't edge as you go you will end up with a daunting pile squares needing to be done one after the other.

Round 1: with right side facing and foundation ch at top (your square should be upside down), join with dc (US sc) in first ch and work 2 dc (US sc) in same ch, then work 24 dc (US sc) evenly across each side with 3 dc (US sc) in each corner ch around, join with ss to first dc (US sc), do not finish off — 108 dc (US sc).

Round 2: 1 ch, dc (US sc) in same st, *3 dc (US sc) in next corner st, dc (US sc) in each st across to next corner st, repeat from * around, join with ss in first dc (US sc), finish off — 116 dc (US sc).

MARKERS

Use markers for easy identification of top and bottom of work and for corner stitches in edging.

FLOATS

A float is a contrasting yarn taken (floated) across the back of groups of stitches to make multi-coloured patterns. Be careful with consistency here and try to keep the same tension—where floats vary, and are too long, too loose or too tight, they will influence the look of the stitch.

BLOCKING

In most cases blocking is essential in tricot crochet. However, it must be done *carefully*, as this fabric has a tendency to pull on the bias. To help retain textured patterns block on the wrong side, and when using synthetic yarns keep heat as low as possible.

The usual method is to place the square on a terry towel over a flat surface and, using stainless steel pins, secure it to shape, lightly steam and allow to dry *completely* before removing pins.

The alternative, which I recommend over the conventional method, is to pin the square into shape (use stainless steel pins only) and spray liberally with a spray starch. Again, let the square dry *completely* before removing pins.

CHANGING COLOUR AND JOINING YARN

Which end of the row to change colour will depend on what effect you are after. Make small swatches of 16 ch and try out some colour variations before you start your project:

- changing from the right usually results in an even stripe.

- changing from the left gives a more 'tweedy' look to your work.

- a combination of the two will produce interesting effects also.

- introducing new colours mid row and/or using floats will create even more options.

JOINING NEW COLOUR AT END OF ROW FROM THE LEFT (END OF PICK-UP ROW)

With last loop completed, drop old colour, make a ss on hook with new colour and draw through (this counts as 1 ch), continue by drawing new colour through 2 loops as usual.

CHANGING COLOUR ALREADY IN USE FROM LEFT

With last loop completed, drop old colour, float new colour up by drawing up a loop (this counts as 1 ch), continue by drawing new colour through 2 loops as usual.

JOINING NEW COLOUR AT END OF ROW FROM RIGHT (END OF CAST-OFF ROW)

When 2 loops remain on hook, drop old colour, draw new colour through 2 loops. This new loop becomes the first stitch of the next row. It isn't anchored so be careful keeping your tension firm, and leave a long tail to weave in later.

CHANGING COLOUR ALREADY IN USE FROM RIGHT

When 2 loops remain on hook, drop old colour, float new colour up and draw through 2 loops. This new loop becomes the first stitch of the next row.

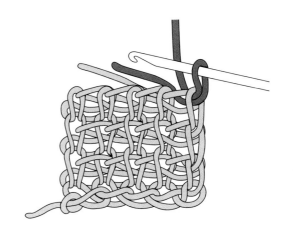

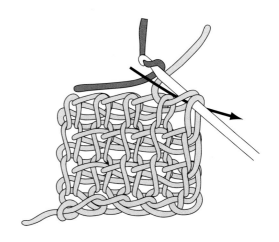

TUNISIAN DIAGRAM SYMBOLS

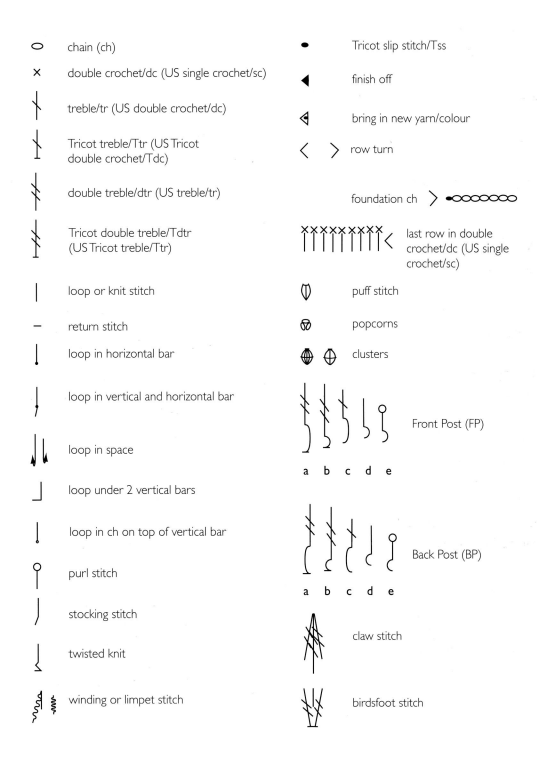

chain (ch)

double crochet/dc (US single crochet/sc)

treble/tr (US double crochet/dc)

Tricot treble/Ttr (US Tricot double crochet/Tdc)

double treble/dtr (US treble/tr)

Tricot double treble/Tdtr (US Tricot treble/Ttr)

loop or knit stitch

return stitch

loop in horizontal bar

loop in vertical and horizontal bar

loop in space

loop under 2 vertical bars

loop in ch on top of vertical bar

purl stitch

stocking stitch

twisted knit

winding or limpet stitch

Tricot slip stitch/Tss

finish off

bring in new yarn/colour

row turn

foundation ch

last row in double crochet/dc (US single crochet/sc)

puff stitch

popcorns

clusters

Front Post (FP)

a   b   c   d   e

Back Post (BP)

a   b   c   d   e

claw stitch

birdsfoot stitch

ABBREVIATIONS

ch	chain
ss	slip stitch
dc (US sc)	double crochet (US single crochet)
tr (US dc)	treble (US double crochet)
htr (US hdc)	half treble (US half double crochet)
dtr (US tr)	double treble (US treble)
trtr (US dtr)	triple treble (US double treble)
qtr (US trtr)	quadruple treble (US triple treble)
BPtr (US BPdc)	Back Post treble (US Back Post double crochet)
FPtr (US FPdc)	Front Post treble (US Front Post double crochet)
FPhtr (US FPhdc)	Front Post half treble (US Front Post half double crochet)
Tss	Tricot slip stitch/
YO	yarn over
sp	space
st	stitch

TRICOT STITCH GUIDE

Treble/tr (US double crochet/dc)
(one ch is needed at beginning of row when working in trebles)

YO, insert hook under vertical bar or into st indicated, YO, draw up a loop, YO and draw through 2 loops leaving 1 loop on hook.

Double treble/dtr (US treble/tr)
(2 ch are needed at beginning of row when working in double trebles)

YO twice, insert hook under vertical bar or into st indicated, YO, draw up a loop, (YO and draw through 2 loops) twice, leaving 1 loop on hook.

For extra height and a more open weave, work trebles (US double crochet) and double trebles (US trebles) as follows:

Trebles (US double crochet): (1 ch at beginning of row) YO, insert hook under vertical bar or into st indicated, YO, draw up a loop, YO and draw through 1 loop, YO and draw through 2 loops, leaving 1 loop on hook.

Double trebles (US trebles): (2 ch at beginning of row) YO twice, insert hook under vertical bar or into st indicated, YO, draw up a loop, YO and draw through 2 loops, YO and draw through 1 loop, YO and draw through 2 loops, leaving 1 loop on hook.

SPECIAL TRICOT STITCHES

Tricot stitches differ from basic stitches by being anchored before completing the stitch.

Tricot treble/Ttr (US Tricot double crochet/ Tdc)

Insert hook under next vertical bar and draw up a loop, YO, insert hook under vertical bar indicated, YO and draw up a loop, (YO and draw through 2 loops) twice.

Tricot double treble/Tdtr (US Tricot trebles/Ttr)

Insert hook under next vertical bar and draw up a loop, YO twice, insert hook under vertical bar indicated, YO and draw up a loop, YO and draw through 2 loops, YO and draw through 3 loops.

● **Tricot slip stitch/Tss**
Pick up vertical bar, *do not* draw through a loop.

I recommend making swatches as practice to master the stitches. The squares do not always follow the swatch pattern completely, but show how the stitch can be utilised in one or two colours and how stitch sequences can be changed to create different effects.

SWATCH 1:
BASIC TRICOT STITCH (BT)

PATTERN

Foundation chain: using ordinary hook, make any number of ch as required. Change to Tunisian hook.

Row 1a: (pick-up row) insert hook in next ch, draw up a loop and leave on hook, repeat across to end — same number of loops on hook as foundation ch.

Row 1b: (cast-off row) YO, draw through first loop on hook, *YO, draw through 2 loops on hook, repeat from * across until one loop remains (this last loop is the first loop of the next pick-up row).

These first two rows form the basis of most tricot stitches and will be referred to throughout this section as a row of BT.

Notice how Row 1a has formed vertical bars; from now on the hook is inserted through these bars (unless otherwise stated in pattern). Because the first stitch of this row is already on the hook, skip the first vertical bar (the one directly below loop) and insert hook into 2nd bar.

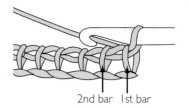

2nd bar   1st bar

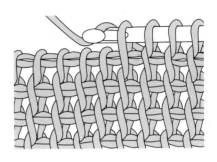

Knit stitch (BT) is an ideal base for embroidery, cross-stitch and other decorative needlework.

Row 2a: *insert hook under next vertical bar, YO and draw up a loop, repeat from * across to last vertical bar — same number of loops on hook as foundation ch.

Row 2b: cast off as in BT.

Repeat Rows 2a and 2b to desired size, changing to ordinary hook for last row.

SQUARE 1:
KNIT STITCH (BT) IN ONE COLOUR

Make 26 ch and work rows of BT to desired size.

Edging: refer to Edging for Tricot squares, page 119.

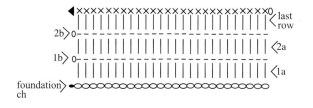

SQUARE 2:
KNIT STITCH IN TWO COLOURS

Make 26 ch, beginning with Col-A and, changing colour from the *left*, work 1 row of each colour in knit st to desired size.

Edging: refer to Edging the squares, page 119.

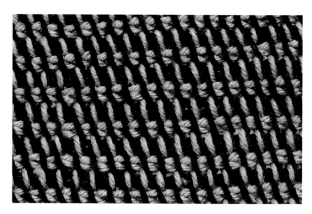

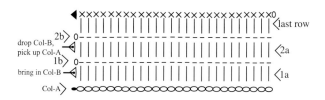

SWATCH 2:
STOCKING STITCH

This is an easy and versatile stitch which lends itself as a background for popcorns, clusters and other texture stitches.

PATTERN

Foundation chain: using ordinary hook, make any number of ch as required. Change to Tunisian hook.

Foundation row: make 1 row of BT.

Row 2a: *insert hook through centre of next vertical bar, YO, draw up a loop and leave on hook, repeat from * across to last vertical bar — same number of loops on hook as foundation ch.

Row 2b: cast off as in BT.

Repeat Rows 2a and 2b to desired size, changing to ordinary hook for last row.

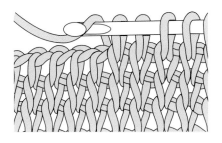

SQUARE 3:
STOCKING STITCH IN TWO COLOURS

Make 26 ch beginning with Col-A and, changing colour from the *right*, work 2 rows of each colour in stocking st to desired size.

Edging: refer to Edging the squares, page 119.

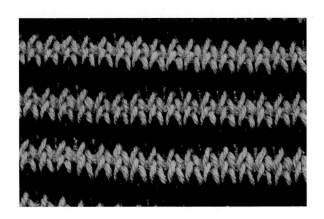

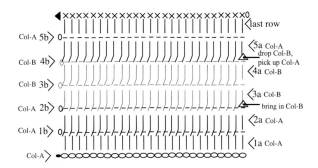

SWATCH 3:
PURL STITCH

Purl stitch is not particularly attractive on its own but is a necessary stitch to know as it forms part of many stitch combinations.

PATTERN

Foundation chain: using ordinary hook, make any number of ch as required. Change to Tunisian hook.

Foundation row: make one row of BT. From now on the yarn is held in *front* of work.

Row 2a: *insert hook under next vertical bar, YO, draw up a loop and leave on hook, repeat from * across to last vertical bar — same number of loops on hook as foundation ch.

Row 2b: cast off as in BT.

Repeat Rows 2a and 2b to desired size, changing to ordinary hook for last row.

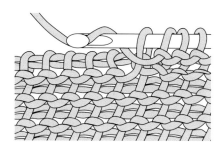

SQUARE 4:
PURL STITCH IN ONE COLOUR

Make 26 ch and work rows of purl st to desired size.

Edging: refer to Edging the squares, page 119.

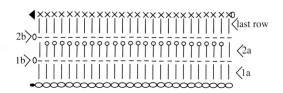

SWATCH 4:
DOUBLE KNIT STITCH

PATTERN

Foundation chain: using ordinary hook, make any number of ch as required. Change to Tunisian hook.

Foundation row: make one row of BT.

Row 2a: *insert hook under next vertical bar, YO and draw up a loop, 1 ch through loop just made, repeat from * to across last vertical bar, insert hook through turning ch, YO and draw up a loop through both loops — same number of loops on hook as foundation ch

Row 2b: cast off as in BT.

Repeat Rows 2a and 2b to desired size, changing to ordinary hook for last row.

SQUARE 5:
DOUBLE KNIT STITCH IN TWO COLOURS
Make 26 ch beginning with Col-A and, changing colour from the *left*, work 1 row of each colour in double knit st to desired size.

Edging: refer to Edging the squares, page 119.

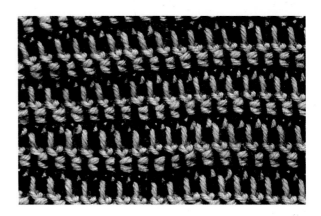

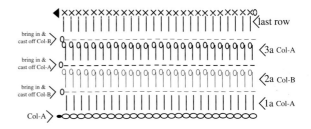

SWATCH 5:
SOLID KNIT STITCH

This stitch has regular straight bars and is an ideal base for embroidery, cross-stitch and other decorative needlework.

Work in vertical and horizontal bars

PATTERN

Foundation chain: using ordinary hook, make any number of ch as required. Change to Tunisian hook.

Foundation row: make one row of BT.

Row 2a: *insert hook under next vertical and horizontal bar, YO and draw up a loop, repeat from * to last vertical bar — same number of loops on hook as foundation ch.

Row 2b: cast off as in BT.

Repeat Rows 2a and 2b to desired size, changing to ordinary hook for last row.

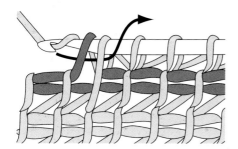

SQUARE 6:
SOLID KNIT STITCH IN ONE COLOUR

Make 26 ch then follow pattern for solid knit st to desired size.

Edging: refer to Edging the squares, page 119.

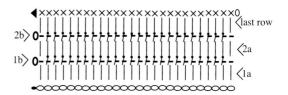

SWATCH 6:
SOLID KNIT STITCH AND TDTR (US TTR) CABLE STITCH

Tricot double treble/Tdtr (US Tricot treble/Ttr)
see special tricot stitches (page 122)

after Row 5a, Tdtr (US Ttr) are worked around Front Post (FP) of Tdtr (US Ttr) 4 rows below.

Front Post Tricot double treble/FPTdtr (US Front Post Tricot treble/FPTtr)

PATTERN

Foundation chain: using ordinary hook, make number of ch in multiples of 2 as required. Change to Tunisian hook.

Foundation row: make 1 row of BT.

Rows 2, 3 and 4: make 3 rows of solid knit st.

Row 5a: *solid knit st under next 3 vertical bars (4 loops on hook and count as 4 solid knit sts), work Tdtr (US Ttr) under next 2 vertical bars 4 rows below, repeat from * to last vertical bar — same number of loops on hook as foundation ch.

Row 5b: cast off as in BT.

Rows 6a to 8b: make 3 rows of solid knit st.

Row 9a: *solid knit st under next 3 vertical bars, work FPTdtr (US FPTtr) around Tdtr (US Ttr) 4 rows below, repeat from * to last vertical bar — same number of loops on hook as foundation ch.

Row 9b: cast off as in BT.

Rows 10a to 12b: make 3 rows of solid knit st.

Repeat Rows 2a to 12b to desired size, changing to ordinary hook for last row.

SQUARE 7:
SOLID KNIT STITCH AND TDTR (US TTR) CABLE STITCH IN ONE COLOUR

Make 26 ch, 1 row BT, then work 3 rows in solid knit st (4 rows made).

Row 5a: use diagram as guide for Tdtr (US Ttr) placement. Repeat to required depth.

Edging: refer to Edging the squares, page 119.

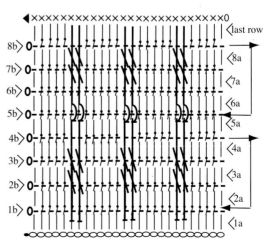

SWATCH 7:
RIPPLE-WAVE STITCH

Note: In this pattern Col-B refers to main colour and Col-A to contrast colour.

- Tss (Tricot slip stitch)

knit stitch

treble (US double crochet)

PATTERN

Foundation chain: using ordinary hook and Col-A, make number of ch in multiples of 2 as required. Change to Tunisian hook.

Foundation row: with Col-A make one row of BT, changing to Col-B in last 2 loops.

Row 2a: continuing with Col-B work *1 knit st (2 loops on hook and counts as 2 knit sts), 2 Tss, 2 knit st, 4 tr, repeat from * to last vertical bar — same number of loops on hook as foundation ch.

Row 2b: cast off as in BT, changing to Col-A in last 2 loops.

Row 3: continuing with Col-A make one row of BT, changing to Col-B in last 2 loops.

Row 4a: continuing with Col-B work *4 tr, 2 knit st, 2 Tss, 2 knit st, repeat from * to last vertical bar — same number of loops on hook as foundation ch.

Row 4b: cast off as in BT, changing to Col-A in last 2 loops.

Row 5: continuing with Col-A make one row of BT, changing to Col-B in last 2 loops.

Repeat Rows 2a to 5 to desired size, changing to ordinary hook for last row.

SQUARE 8:
RIPPLE-WAVE STITCH IN TWO COLOURS

Make 26 ch and using diagram as guide for st placement work rows of ripple-wave st to desired size.

Edging: refer to Edging the squares, page 119.

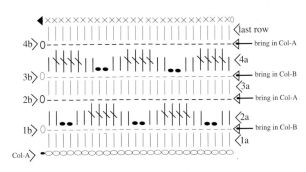

SWATCH 8:
TREBLES (US DOUBLE CROCHET)

Trebles/tr (US double crochet/dc)

PATTERN

Foundation chain: using ordinary hook, make any number of ch as required. Change to Tunisian hook.

Foundation row: make one row of BT.

Row 2a: 1 ch, work tr (US dc) under each vertical bar across to last vertical bar — same number of loops on hook as foundation ch.

Row 2b: cast off as in BT.

Repeat Rows 2a and 2b to desired size, changing to ordinary hook for last row.

SQUARE 9:
TREBLES IN ONE COLOUR

Make 26 ch then follow pattern for trebles (US double crochet) to desired size.

Edging: refer to Edging the squares, page 119.

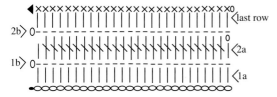

SWATCH 9:
CROSS STITCH

Cross stitch is both attractive on its own and necessary to know as it forms part of many stitch combinations.

The pairs of stitches are worked in reverse order.

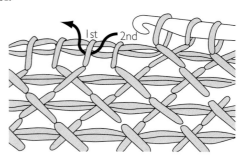

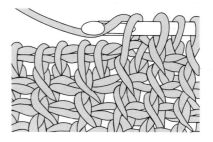

PATTERN

Foundation chain: using ordinary hook, make number of ch in multiples of 2 as required. Change to Tunisian hook.

Foundation row: make one row of BT.

Row 2a: *skip next vertical bar, insert hook under next vertical bar, YO, draw up a loop and leave on hook, insert hook from right to left under skipped vertical bar, YO, draw up a loop and leave on hook, repeat from * across to last vertical bar — same number of loops on hook as foundation ch.

Row 2b: cast off as in BT.

Repeat Rows 2a and 2b to desired size, changing to ordinary hook for last row.

SQUARE 10:
CROSS STITCH IN ONE COLOUR

Make 26 ch then follow pattern for cross st to desired size.

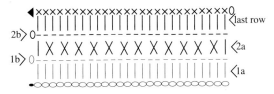

SQUARE 11:
CROSS STITCH IN TWO COLOURS

With Col-B make 26 ch and 1 row BT.

Row 2a: pick up in Col-B.

Row 2b: cast off Col-B, changing to Col-A in last 2 loops — cut off Col-B.

Row 3a: pick up in Col-A — cut off Col-A.

Row 3b: cast off in Col-B.

Row 4a: pick up in Col-B in cross st.

Row 4b: cast off in Col-B.

Row 5a: pick up in Col-B.

Row 5b: cast off Col-B, changing to Col-A in last 2 loops — cut off Col-B.

Repeat Rows 2a to 5b to desired size.

Edging: refer to Edging the squares, page 119.

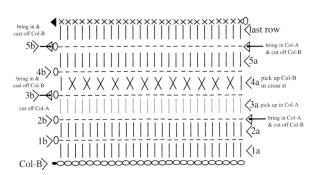

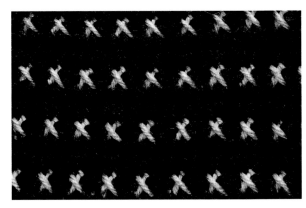

SWATCH 10:
MOSS STITCH

Moss stitch looks much like knitting—it is firm and neat on both sides but does require concentration in alternating sts and rows.

PATTERN

Work knit and purl sts alternately in each row, then alternately over the previous row.

Foundation chain: using ordinary hook, make any number of ch as required. Change to Tunisian hook.

Foundation row: make one row of BT.

Row 2a: *1 purl st under next vertical bar, 1 knit st under next vertical bar, repeat from * across to last vertical bar — same number of loops on hook as foundation ch.

Row 2b: cast off as in BT.

Row 3a: *1 knit st under next vertical bar, 1 purl st under next vertical bar, repeat from * across to last vertical bar — same number of loops on hook as foundation ch.

Row 3b: cast off as in BT.

Repeat Rows 2a to 3b to desired size, changing to ordinary hook for last row.

SQUARE 12:
MOSS STITCH IN ONE COLOUR

Make 26 ch and follow moss st pattern to desired size.

Edging: refer to Edging the squares, page 119.

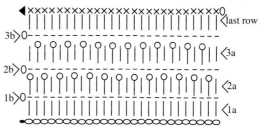

SQUARE 13:
MOSS STITCH IN TWO COLOURS

Beginning with Col-A, make 26 ch, then following moss st pattern and changing colour from the *right*, work 1 row of each colour to desired size, changing to ordinary hook for last row.

Edging: refer to Edging the squares, page 119.

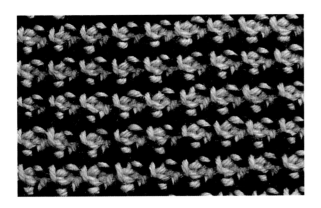

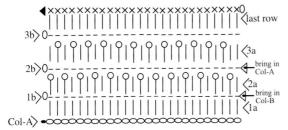

SWATCH 11:
STOCKING STITCH AND BACK POST PURL RIB STITCH

Rib stitches can be worked in endless combinations, so try a few different ones and discover which you prefer. (For example, ribs consisting of 4 sts would require chains of 16, 40, 80 and so on.)

The directions for this pattern are given in multiples of 3 (3 stocking st, 3 purl st).

Back Post purl: with yarn at back of work and working in the sps between sts, insert hook from *back* to *front* around both vertical bars of next st, YO, draw through a loop and leave on hook.

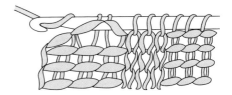

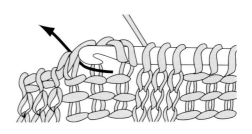

PATTERN

Foundation chain: using ordinary hook, make ch in multiples of 3 as required for number of stitches in each rib. Change to Tunisian hook.

Foundation row: make one row of BT.

Row 2a: *stocking st in next 2 vertical bars, BP purl st around next 3 vertical bars, repeat from * across to last vertical bar — same number of loops on hook as foundation ch.

Row 2b: cast off as in BT.

Repeat Rows 2a and 2b to desired size, changing to ordinary hook for last row.

SQUARE 14:
STOCKING STITCH AND BACK POST PURL RIB IN TWO COLOURS

Beginning with Col-A, make 26 ch and, using diagram as guide for st placement, follow pattern, changing colour from the *right* and working 1 row of each colour to desired size.

Edging: refer to Edging the squares, page 119.

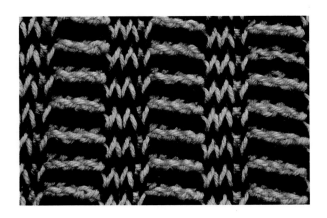

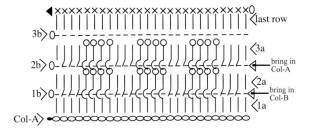

SWATCH 12:
KNIT AND PURL RIB

Knit and purl rib is easy and versatile and can be worked in endless combinations, so try a few to work out which you prefer. (For example, ribs consisting of 4 sts would require chains of 16, 40, 80 and so on.)

The directions for this pattern are given in multiples of 3 (3 knit st, 3 purl st).

PATTERN

Foundation chain: using ordinary hook, make ch in multiples of 3 as required for number of stitches in each rib. Change to Tunisian hook.

Foundation row: make one row of BT.

Row 2a: *knit st under next 2 vertical bars, purl st under next 3 vertical bars, repeat from * across to last vertical bar — same number of loops on hook as foundation ch.

Row 2b: cast off as in BT.

Repeat Rows 2a and 2b to desired size, changing to ordinary hook for last row.

SQUARE 15:
KNIT AND PURL RIB IN ONE COLOUR

Make 26 ch and follow pattern using diagram as guide for st placement.

Edging: refer to Edging the squares, page 119.

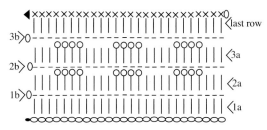

SWATCH 13:
TRICOT BASKET WEAVE STITCH

PATTERN

Foundation chain: using ordinary hook, make number of ch in multiples of 8 + 4 as required. Change to Tunisian hook.

Foundation row: make one row of BT.

Rows 2a: *stocking st in next 3 vertical bars (4 loops on hook and count as 4 stocking sts), purl sts under next 4 vertical bars, repeat from * across to end — same number of loops on hook as foundation ch.

Row 2b: cast off as in BT.

Row 3a: repeat Row 2a.

Row 3b: cast off as in BT.

Row 4a: repeat Row 2a.

Row 4b: cast off as in BT.

Row 5a: repeat Row 2a.

Row 5b: cast off as in BT.

Rows 6a: *purl st under next 3 vertical bars (4 loops on hook and count as 4 purl sts), stocking st in next 4 vertical bars, repeat from * across to end — same number of loops on hook as foundation ch.

Row 6b: cast off as in BT.

Row 7a: repeat Row 6a.

Row 7b: cast off as in BT.

Row 8a: repeat Row 6a.

Row 8b: cast off as in BT.

Row 9a: repeat Row 6a.

Row 9b: cast off as in BT.

Repeat Rows 2a to 9b to desired size, changing to ordinary hook for last row.

SQUARE 16:
TRICOT BASKET WEAVE STITCH IN ONE COLOUR

Make 26 ch and use diagram as guide for st placement.

Edging: refer to Edging the squares, page 119.

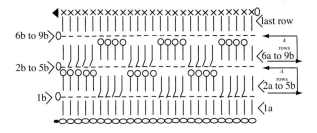

SWATCH 14:
CHENILLE STITCH

This stitch is worked in the chain at the top of vertical bar on working row and under vertical bars of 2 rows below.

PATTERN

Foundation chain: using ordinary hook, make any number of ch as required. Change to Tunisian hook.

Foundation row: make 2 rows of BT.

Row 3a: *insert hook under next 2 vertical bars 2 rows below and draw up a loop, 1 ch in loop just made and leave on hook, insert hook through next ch on top of vertical bar and draw up a loop, repeat from * to last vertical bar — same number of loops on hook as foundation ch.

Row 3b: cast off as in BT.

Row 4: make one row of BT.

Repeat Rows 3a to 4b to desired size, changing to ordinary hook for last row.

SQUARE 17:
CHENILLE STITCH IN ONE COLOUR

Make 26 ch and follow chenille st pattern.

Edging: refer to Edging the squares, page 119.

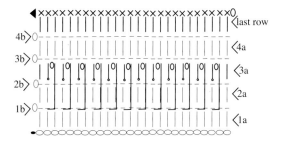

SQUARE 18:
CHENILLE STITCH IN TWO COLOURS

With Col-A make 26 ch.

Foundation row: make 1 row of BT and one extra pick-up row (pick-up row becomes Row 2a).

Row 2b: change to Col-B and cast off.

Row 3a: pick up as for chenille st.

Row 3b: change to Col-A and cast off.

Row 4a: pick up as for BT.

Repeat rows 2b to 4b to desired size.

Edging: refer to Edging the squares, page 119.

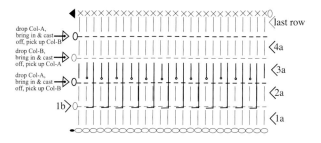

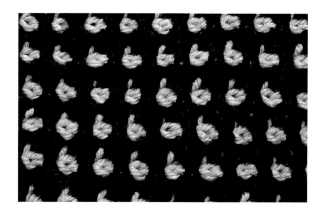

SWATCH 15:
TRICOT OR TUNISIAN
LADDER STITCH

Ladder stitch produces a tightly woven fabric that looks neat on both sides. The YO puts an extra loop on hook which is manually passed over the last 3 loops just made. It is surprisingly easy and quicker than you first expect.

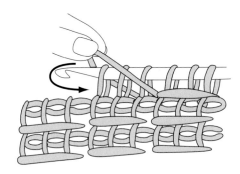

PATTERN

Foundation chain: using ordinary hook, make number of ch in multiples of 3 + 2 as required. Change to Tunisian hook.

Foundation row: make one row of BT.

Row 2a: *YO, work knit st under next 3 vertical bars (5 loops on hook), take the 2nd loop on hook and pass it over the 3 loops just made, repeat from * across to last vertical bar — same number of loops on hook as foundation ch.

Row 2b: cast off as in BT.

Repeat Rows 2a and 2b to desired size, changing to ordinary hook for last row.

SQUARE 19:
LADDER STITCH IN ONE COLOUR

Make 26 ch and, using graph for st placement, work rows of ladder st to desired size.

Edging: refer to Edging the squares, page 119.

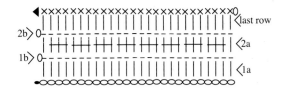

SQUARE 20:
LADDER STITCH IN TWO COLOURS

Beginning with Col-A and using ordinary hook, make 26 ch. Change to Tunisian hook. Using diagram for st placement, work 1 row of each colour in ladder st, changing colour from the left, to desired size, changing to ordinary hook for last row.

Edging: refer to Edging for Tricot squares, page 119.

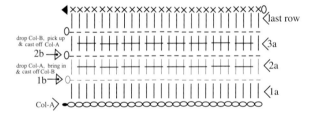

SWATCH 16:
WAFFLE STITCH

This stitch has a tendency to go off to the left. To alleviate this, skip the first space on alternate rows and keep a close count of stitches at end of each pick-up row. Waffle stitch is quick and easy but concentration is needed when alternating rows.

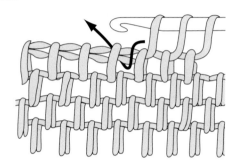

PATTERN

Foundation chain: using ordinary hook, make any number of ch as required. Change to Tunisian hook.

Foundation row: make one row of BT.

Row 2a: *insert hook in sp between next vertical bars, YO, draw up a loop and leave on hook, repeat from * across to end — same number of loops on hook as foundation ch.

Row 2b: cast off as in BT.

Row 3a: skip first sp, *insert hook in sp between next vertical bars, YO, draw up a loop and leave on hook, repeat from * across to last vertical bar — same number of loops on hook as foundation ch.

Row 3b: cast off as in BT.

Repeat Rows 2a to 3b to desired size, changing to ordinary hook for last row.

SQUARE 21:
WAFFLE STITCH IN TWO COLOURS

Beginning with Col-A and using ordinary hook, make 26 ch, change to Tunisian hook. Following pattern for waffle st and changing colour from the *right*, work 1 row of each colour to desired size, changing to ordinary hook for last row.

Edging: refer to Edging the squares, page 119.

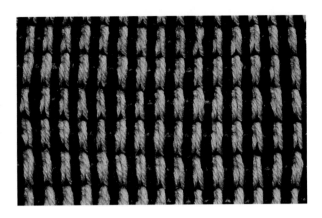

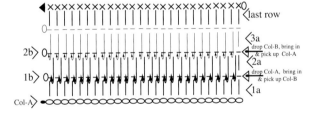

SWATCH 17:
TRICOT TRIANGLE STITCH

Twisted knit stitch: with hook sitting over next vertical bar, move hook from left to right, pick up bar while twisting the hook upwards, YO and draw up a loop (twisted knit stitch made).

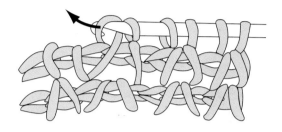

PATTERN

Foundation chain: using ordinary hook, make any number of ch as required. Change to Tunisian hook.

Foundation row: make one row of BT.

Row 2a: *1 knit st, 1 twisted knit st, repeat from * to last vertical bar — same number of loops on hook as foundation ch.

Row 2b: cast off as in BT.

Repeat Rows 2a and 2b to desired size, changing to ordinary hook for last row.

SQUARE 22:
ALIGNED TRICOT TRIANGLES IN TWO COLOURS

Beginning with Col-A make 26 ch.

Row 1a and 1b: with Col-A make one row of BT.

Row 2a: pick up with Col-A.

Row 2b: cast off with Col-B.

Row 3a: pick up with Col-B, *1 twisted knit st, 1 knit st, repeat from * across to end.

Row 3b: cast off with Col-A.

Repeat rows 2a to 3b to desired size.

Edging: refer to Edging the squares, page 119.

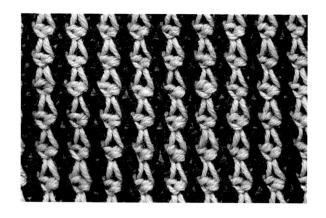

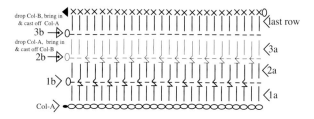

SWATCH 18:
RELIEF TREBLE AND DOUBLE TREBLE COMBINATIONS

There are hundreds of combinations for relief trebles and double trebles; the patterns given here are only a few.

Ttr (US Tdc) see Special Abbreviations

Tdtr (US Ttr) see Special Abbreviations

Ttr (US Tdc) requires 3 foundation rows of BT

Tdtr (US Ttr) requires 4 foundation rows of BT

PATTERN

Foundation chain: using ordinary hook, make even number of ch as required. Change to Tunisian hook.

Foundation rows 1 to 4: make 4 rows of BT.

Row 5a: *1 knit st (2 loops on hook and count as 2 knit sts), work Tdtr (US Ttr) under next vertical bar directly 4 rows below, repeat from * to last vertical bar — same number of loops on hook as foundation ch.

Row 5b: cast off as in BT.

Rows 6 and 7: make 2 rows of BT.

Row 8a: *work Tdtr (US Ttr) under next vertical bar directly 4 rows below, 2 knit sts, repeat from * to last vertical bar — same number of loops on hook as foundation ch.

Row 8b: cast off as in BT.

Rows 9 and 10: make 2 rows of BT.

Repeat Rows 5a to 10b to desired size, changing to ordinary hook for last row.

SQUARE 23:
RELIEF TREBLES IN ONE COLOUR
With Col-A make 26 ch and use pattern diagram as guide for st placement.

Edging: refer to Edging the squares, page 119.

SQUARE 24:
RELIEF DOUBLE TREBLES IN TWO COLOURS
With Col-B make 26 ch and, using pattern diagram as guide for st placement, work double trebles as floats with Col-A.

Edging: refer to Edging for Tricot squares, page 119.

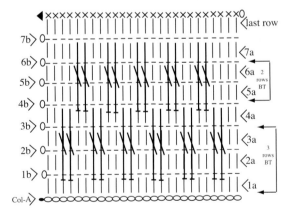

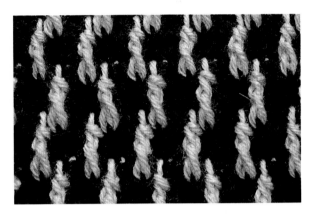

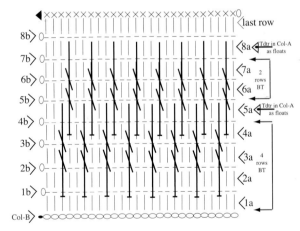

SWATCH 19:
BIRDSFOOT STITCH

This stitch is made up of 2 Tdtr (US Ttr) (see below). Both are worked in the *same st 4 rows below*, with 1 knit st between—keep close count of sts. Instructions are given for a square in an aligned pattern in one colour, and for a square in a staggered pattern in two colours.

 Birdsfoot stitch: work the 2 Tdtr (US Ttr) as follows:

1st Tdtr (US Ttr): work Tdtr (US Ttr) under vertical bar 4 rows below and 1 st forward

1 knit st under next vertical bar of working row

2nd Tdtr (US Ttr): work under *same* vertical bar on 4th row below as in first Tdtr (US Ttr).

PATTERN

Foundation chain: using ordinary hook, make number of ch in multiples of 2 as required. Change to Tunisian hook.

Foundation rows 1a to 4b: make 4 rows of BT.

Row 5a: *1 knit st (2 loops on hook and count as 2 knit sts), work birdsfoot st, repeat from * to last vertical bar — same number of loops on hook as foundation ch.

Row 5b: cast off as in BT

Rows 6, 7 and 8: make 3 rows of BT.

Repeat Rows 5a to 8b to desired size, changing to ordinary hook for last row.

SQUARE 25:
BIRDSFOOT STITCH IN ONE COLOUR

With Col-A make 26 ch, follow pattern and diagram for aligned birdsfoot st to desired size.

Edging: refer to Edging the squares, page 119.

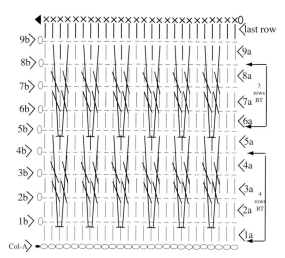

SQUARE 26:
BIRDSFOOT STITCH IN TWO COLOURS

With Col-B make 26 ch and, using pattern diagram as guide for st placement, work staggered birdsfoot st as floats with Col-A to desired size.

*Work first (US Ttr) in col-A, knit st in col-B, 2nd Tdtr (US Ttr) in col-A.

Edging: refer to Edging the squares, page 119.

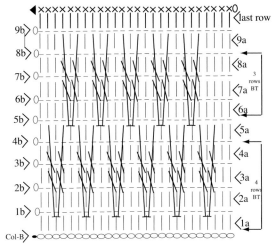

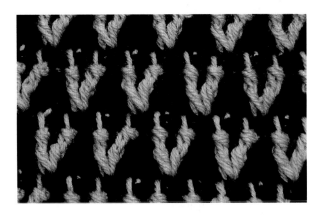

SWATCH 20:
TRICOT POPCORN STITCH

Popcorns are a quick way of bringing texture to your work and can easily be enlarged by increasing the number of chains. Popcorns can be worked on any basic st (knit, stocking, between crosses, for example). Spacing can be also be varied by adjusting the number of sts between each popcorn. Popcorns work well when using floats.

In the pattern given here, stocking st is used as the base st and the popcorns are staggered.

PATTERN

Foundation chain: using ordinary hook, make any number of ch as required. Change to Tunisian hook.

Foundation row: make one row of BT.

Row 2a: *stocking st in next 3 vertical bars (4 loops on hook and counts as 4 stocking sts), 4 ch, repeat from * across to last vertical bar — same number of loops on hook as foundation ch.

Row 2b: cast off as in BT.

Row 3a: *stocking st in next 2 vertical bars (3 loops on hook and counts as 3 stocking sts), 4 ch, repeat from * across to last vertical bar — same number of loops on hook as foundation ch.

Row 3b: cast off as in BT.

Repeat Rows 2a to 3b to desired size, changing to ordinary hook for last row.

SQUARE 27:
POPCORNS IN ONE COLOUR
Make 26 ch.

Row 1: one row of BT.

Row 2a: *stocking st in next 2 vertical bars (3 loops on hook and counts as 3 stocking sts), 4 ch, repeat across to last vertical bar.

Row 2b: cast off as in BT.

Row 3: make one row of stocking st.

Row 3b: cast off as in BT.

Repeat Rows 2a to 3b to desired size.

Edging: refer to Edging the squares, page 119.

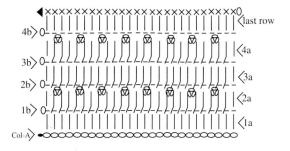

SQUARE 28:
POPCORNS IN TWO COLOURS
With Col-B make 26 ch.

Row 1: continuing with Col-B make one row of BT.

Row 2a: working in knit st and using pattern diagram as guide for st placement, work popcorns as floats with Col-A.

Row 2b: cast off as in BT.

Row 3: make one row of knit st.

Row 3b: cast off as in BT.

Repeat Rows 2a to 3b to desired size.

Edging: refer to Edging the squares, page 119.

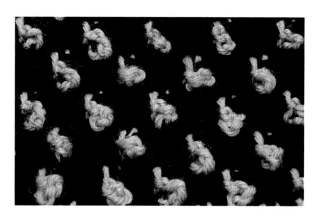

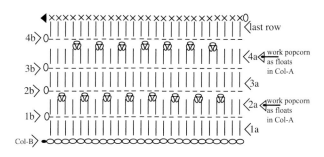

SWATCH 21:
TRICOT PUFF STITCH

Tricot puff stitch: draw up a loop under the next vertical bar, (YO, insert hook under the same vertical bar, YO and draw up a loop) twice, YO, draw through 5 loops just made, 1 ch to close (Tricot puff made).

Purl stitch: when making the purl st directly after the puff, work behind puff with yarn in front. Try to work puffs loosely and keep close count of sts.

PATTERN

Foundation chain: using ordinary hook, make number of ch in multiples of 4 + 2 as required. Change to Tunisian hook.

Foundation row: make 2 rows of BT.

Row 3a: 1 knit st (2 loops on hook), *work puff, 1 purl st, 2 knit sts, repeat from * across to last vertical bar — same number of loops on hook as foundation ch.

Row 3b: cast off as in BT.

Rows 4 and 5: 2 rows of BT.

Row 6a: 3 knit st (4 loops on hook), *work puff, 1 purl st, 2 knit sts, repeat from * across to last vertical bar — same number of loops on hook as foundation ch.

Row 6b: cast off as in BT.

Rows 7 and 8: 2 rows of BT.

Repeat Rows 3 to 8 to desired size, changing to ordinary hook for last row.

SQUARE 29:
PUFF STITCH IN TWO COLOURS

With Col-B make 26 ch.

Rows 1 to 5: continuing with Col-B work 5 rows of BT.

Row 6a: working in knit st and using graph as guide for st placement, work puffs as floats with Col-A.

Row 6b: cast off as in BT.

Rows 7 and 8: 2 rows of knit st.

Repeat Rows 6a to 8b four times more, then make 3 extra rows of knit st.

Edging: refer to Edging the squares, page 119.

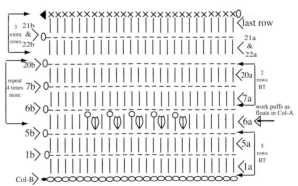

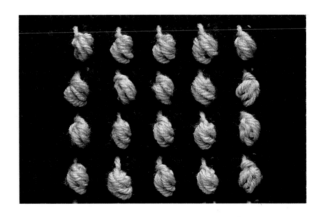

SWATCH 22:
TRICOT BRICKS AND BOXES

The pattern as I give it here is for boxes, but bricks are easily made by off-centring the Tdtr (US Ttr) on alternate rows.

Tdtr (US Ttr) See Special tricot stitches, page 122.

PATTERN

Foundation chain: using ordinary hook, make number of ch in multiples of 3 + 2 as required. Change to Tunisian hook.

Foundation row: with Col-B make one row of BT, changing to Col-A in last 2 loops.

Rows 2 and 3: continuing with Col-A make 2 rows of BT, changing to Col-B in last 2 loops.

Row 4a: continuing with Col-B, 1 knit st (2 loops on hook), work Tdtr (US Ttr) under next vertical bar directly 3 rows below (in Col-B row), *3 knit sts, work Tdtr (US Ttr), repeat from * to last vertical bar — same number of loops on hook as foundation ch.

Row 4b: cast off as in BT, changing to Col-A in last 2 loops.

Rows 5 and 6: continuing with Col-A make 2 rows of BT, changing to Col-B in last 2 loops.

Row 7a: continuing with Col-B, 2 knit sts (3 loops on hook), work Tdtr (US Ttr) under next vertical bar directly 3 rows below (in Col-B row), *3 knit sts, work Tdtr (US Ttr), repeat from * to last vertical bar — same number of loops on hook as foundation ch.

Row 7b: cast off as in BT, changing to Col-A in last 2 loops.

Repeat Rows 1 to 7b to desired size, changing to ordinary hook for last row.

SQUARE 30:
TRICOT BOXES IN TWO COLOURS

With Col-A make 26 ch.

Row 1: continuing with Col-A make one row of BT, changing to Col-B in last 2 loops.

Rows 2, 3 and 4: continuing with Col-B make 3 rows of knit st, changing to Col-A in last 2 loops.

Row 5a: continuing with Col-A and using pattern diagram as guide for st placement, work Tdtr (US Ttr) directly 4 rows below. (The Col-A Tdtr [US tr] is worked 4 rows below the Row 1 Col-A, thus giving the box pattern.)

Row 5b: cast off as in BT, changing to Col-B in last 2 loops.

Repeat Rows 2a to 5b to desired size.

Edging: refer to Edging the squares, page 119.

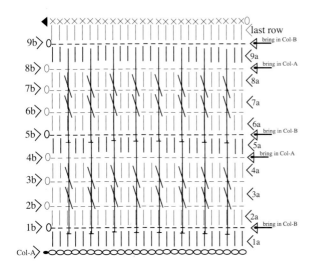

SWATCH 23:
TRICOT CLUSTER STITCH

⊕ **Tricot cluster stitch:** YO, draw up a loop under the next vertical bar, YO, draw through 2 loops, (YO, insert hook under the same vertical bar and draw up a loop, YO and draw through 2 loops) three times, YO, draw through 4 loops just made (Tricot cluster made).

○ **Purl stitch:** when making purl st directly after cluster, work *behind* cluster with yarn in *front*, keeping a close count of sts.

PATTERN

Foundation chain: using ordinary hook, make number of ch in multiples of 4 + 1 as required. Change to Tunisian hook.

Foundation row: make 2 rows of BT.

Row 3a: 1 knit st (2 loops on hook), *work cluster, 1 purl st, 2 knit sts, repeat from * across to last vertical bar — same number of loops on hook as foundation ch.

Row 3b: cast off as in BT.

Rows 4 and 5: 2 rows of BT.

Row 6a: 3 knit sts (4 loops on hook), *work cluster, 1 purl st, 2 knit sts, repeat from * across to last vertical bar — same number of loops on hook as foundation ch.

Row 6b: cast off as in BT.

Rows 7 and 8: 2 rows of BT.

Repeat Rows 3 to 8 to desired size, changing to ordinary hook for last row.

SQUARE 31:
CLUSTER STITCH IN ONE COLOUR

With Col-A make 26 ch.

Row 1: one row of BT.

Row 2a: work in knit st and use diagram as guide for cluster placement.

Row 2b: cast off as for BT.

Row 3a: one row of BT.

Row 3b: cast off as for BT.

Repeat Rows 2a to 3b to desired size.

Edging: refer to Edging the squares, page 119.

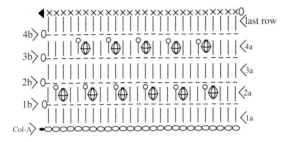

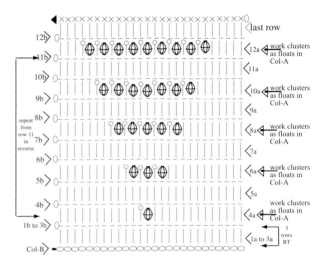

SQUARE 32:
CLUSTER STITCH IN TWO COLOURS

With Col-B make 26 ch.

Row 1, 2 and 3: work 3 rows of BT.

Row 4a and succeeding a rows: working in knit st and using diagram as guide for st placement, work clusters as floats with Col-A.

Row 4b and succeeding b rows: cast off as for BT.

Row 5: one row BT.

Repeat Rows 4a to 5b to desired size.

Edging: refer to Edging the squares, page 119.

SWATCH 24:
ALTERNATE CLAW STITCH

Double treble/dtr (US treble/tr) See special tricot stitches, page 122.

Claw stitch:
1 dtr (US tr) in vertical bar 3 rows below and 1 st back,

1 dtr (US tr) in vertical bar 4 rows below,

1 dtr (US tr) in vertical bar 3 rows below and 1 st forward,

YO, draw through 3 loops (claw st made)

Note: Skip vertical bar directly behind claw st.

PATTERN

Foundation chain: using ordinary hook, make number of ch in multiples of 6 + 2 as required. Change to Tunisian hook.

Foundation rows 1 to 4: continuing with Col-A, make 4 rows of BT, changing to Col-B in last 2 sts of Row 4b.

Row 5a: continuing with Col-B, knit st under next 2 vertical bars (3 loops on hook), *work 1 claw st, knit st under next 5 vertical bars, repeat from * across to last vertical bar — same number of loops on hook as foundation ch.

Row 5b: cast off as in BT, changing to Col-A in last 2 loops.

Row 6 to 9: continuing with Col-A make 4 rows of BT, changing to Col-B in last 2 loops of Row 9b.

Row 10a: continuing with Col-B knit st under next 5 vertical bars (6 loops on hook), *work 1 claw st, knit st under next 5 vertical bars, repeat from * across to last vertical bar — same number of loops on hook as foundation ch.

Row 10b: cast off as in BT, changing to Col-A in last 2 loops.

Repeat Rows 1a to 10b to desired size, changing to ordinary hook for last row.

SQUARE 33:
CLAW STITCH IN ONE COLOUR

Beginning with Col-A make 26 ch and, using diagram for st placement, work rows of claw st to desired size.

Edging: refer to Edging the squares, page 119.

SQUARE 34:
CLAW STITCH IN TWO COLOURS

Beginning with Col-B make 26 ch and, using diagram for st placement, work rows of claw st to desired size.

Edging: refer to Edging for Tricot squares, page 119.

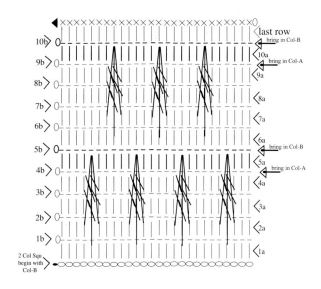

SWATCH 25:
PEBBLE STITCH

Remember that the pebbles should not sit directly on top of each other.

PATTERN

Foundation chain: using ordinary hook, make number of ch in multiples of 2 as required. Change to Tunisian hook.

Foundation row: make one row of BT.

Row 2a: pick up as for BT.

Row 2b: 1 ch, YO and draw through 2 loops, *3 ch, (YO and draw through 2 loops) twice, repeat from * across to end.

Row 3a: working behind 3 ch, pick up as for BT.

Row 3b: 1 ch, (YO and draw through 2 loops) twice, *3 ch, (YO and draw through 2 loops) twice, repeat from * across to end.

Repeat Rows 2a to 3b to desired size, changing to ordinary hook for last row.

SQUARE 35:
PEBBLE STITCH IN ONE COLOUR

Make 26 ch then follow pattern for pebble st to desired size.

Edging: refer to Edging the squares, page 119.

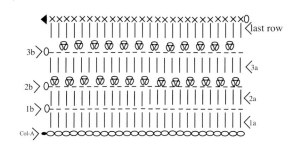

SWATCH 26:
LIMPET STITCH

Limpet stitch is rather slow and fiddly but, with a bit of practice, easier than it looks. Keep limpets well spaced and keep close count of sts. Unless otherwise stated in pattern, always work next bar or st directly behind limpet st on working row.

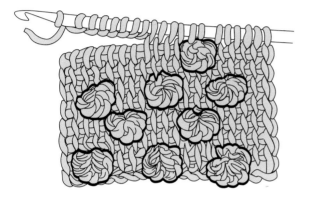

Tricot limpet stitch:
insert hook under vertical bar or into st indicated and draw up a loop, cast on 7 new loops as follows:

work hook (YO) in an anti-clockwise direction, pick up yarn and draw under and through, do this 7 times — 8 loops on hook

YO and draw through all 8 loops

insert hook one st forward on previous row, YO and draw up a loop

YO and draw through 2 loops (the loop of previous row and the loop drawn through the 8), one loop left on hook (limpet stitch made).

Foundation chain: using ordinary hook, make any number of ch as required. Change to Tunisian hook.

Foundation row: make 3 rows of BT.

Row 4a: *2 knit sts (3 loops on hook and count as 3 knit sts), work limpet st, repeat from * to last vertical bar — same number of loops on hook as foundation ch.

Row 4b: cast off as in BT.

Rows 5 and 6: make 2 rows of BT.

Row 7a: *3 knit sts (4 loops on hook and count as 4 knit sts), work limpet st, repeat from * to last vertical bar — same number of loops on hook as foundation ch.

Row 7b: cast off as in BT.

Rows 8 and 9: make 2 rows of BT.

Repeat Rows 4a to 9b to desired size, changing to ordinary hook for last row.

SQUARE 36:
LIMPET STITCH IN ONE COLOUR

With col-A make 26 ch.

Rows 1–3: work 3 rows of BT.

Row 4a: work in knit st and use pattern diagram as guide for limpet placement.

Row 4b: cast off as for BT.

Rows 5 and 6: work 2 rows BT.

Repeat Rows 4a to 7b to desired size.

Edging: refer to Edging the squares, page 119.

FINISHING

JOINING SQUARES

Remember to use an ordinary crochet hook, the same size as used for foundation chain and last row.

Lay out squares according to placement chart or as desired. Pin the squares together, for easier handling working with 2 rows of squares at a time. Take care to always join from the same end for each row being joined.

Working from right to left, with right sides of both squares facing outward, work back loop (centre loops) of both squares, join in first sts using one of the joining methods listed under Techniques at the beginning of the book—invisible join (mattress stitch), visible or flat join (whip stitch), slip stitch join or dc (us sc) join. The dc (US sc) method, which is the strongest, was used for the sampler in the photo.

If you use the slip stitch join or dc (US sc) join, work in Col-C yarn. The dc (US sc) join was used for the rug in the photo.

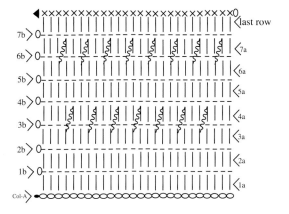

SQUARES PLACEMENT CHART

22	6	5	9	11	10
17	29	33	24	23	18
13	31	8	35	34	19
16	28	7	32	25	2
14	36	26	27	30	15
1	21	4	3	12	20

EDGING
(worked after all squares are joined)

Remember to use an ordinary crochet hook, the same size as used for joining the squares.

Round 1: (work in Col-C and back loops only) join Col-C with dc (US sc) in back loop of any corner st, 2 dc (US sc) in same st, *dc (US sc) in each st across to next corner st, 3 dc (US sc) in corner st, repeat from * around, join with ss to first dc (US sc), finish off.

Round 2: (work in Col-A and back loops only) join Col-A with ss in back loop of any corner st, 2 ch (counts as first htr [US hdc]), 2 htr in same st (corner made), *htr in each st across to next corner st, 3 htr (US hdc) in corner st, repeat from * around, join with ss to top of beginning ch, finish off.

Round 3: (work in Col-B and both loops) join Col-B with dc (US sc) in both loops of any corner st, 2 dc (US sc) in same st, *dc (US sc) in each st across to next corner st, 3 dc (US sc) in corner st, repeat from * around, join with ss to first dc (US sc), finish off.

Round 4: (work in Col-A and both loops) repeat Round 2.

Round 5: (work in Col-C and both loops; for picot st see below) join Col-C with dc (US sc) in both loops of any corner st, work picot st and 1 dc (US sc) in same st (corner made), *work 3 dc (US sc), 1 picot st, across to next corner st, (1 dc [US sc], 1 picot st, 1 dc [US sc]) in corner st, repeat from * around, join with ss to first dc (US sc), finish off.

Picot stitch Make 1 dc (US sc) in next st, 3 ch, then ss in 3rd ch from hook (picot made).

CROCHENIT SAMPLER RUG

LEVEL: ABOVE AVERAGE TO ADVANCED

A derivative of Tunisian crochet, crochenit, also known as 'on the double crochet', uses a long, double-ended hook that produces an interesting reversible fabric. In most cases, using two or more colours will produce a different colour each side.

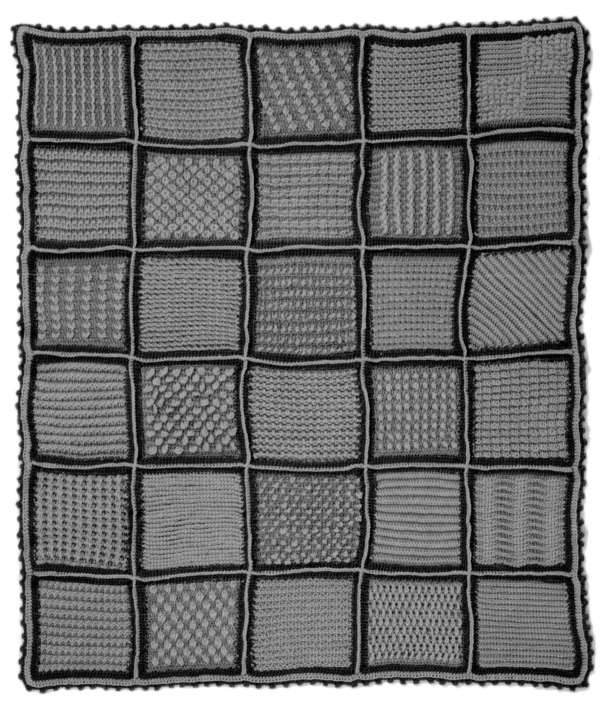

REQUIREMENTS For the rug in the photo I used a 4.50 (US G) double-ended crochet hook for the main part of the squares and a 4.00 (US F) ordinary hook for edging. The three yarns used were (approximately) 350 g of Lincraft Double Knitting 8-ply wool in Light Blue (Col-A), 350 g Lincraft Double Knitting 8-ply wool in Mauve (Col-B), and 250 g Patons Fireside 8-ply wool in Purple (Col-C).

TIPS AND POINTERS

- As a general rule, when working crochenit you turn the work at the end of the pick-up row, and you do not turn at the end of the cast-off row.

- Holding the double-ended hook as you would hold a knife makes your work grow faster and more easily.

- When working with two or more colours, rotate the hook back and forth (clockwise and anti-clockwise) to prevent tangling.

- If you wish to work with yarns that differ from each other, check on their cleaning requirements first.

- Always leave long ends to weave in later.

- Where possible, lay work aside at the end of a pick-up row (when all loops are on hook).

- Be aware that the first loop of the pick-up row is floating; you need to keep the tension of this stitch even for a neater edge finish.

- Markers Loop a short piece of yarn around any stitch to indicate side A (Col-A) and also to easily identify corner stitches in the edging.

BASIC TWO-COLOUR CROCHENIT TECHNIQUE
With Col-A make number of ch as required (foundation chain).

Row 1: Pick-up row
1a: holding double-ended hook like a knife, insert hook in 2nd ch from hook, YO and draw up a loop, leave loop on hook.

1b: *insert hook in next ch, and draw up a loop, leave loop on hook, repeat from * across, leaving all loops on hook (same number of ch on hook as foundation ch),

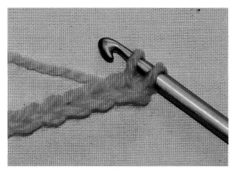

then drop Col-A, turn hook and slide all loops to opposite end of hook (each loop counts as a stitch called a vertical bar).

Row 2: Cast-off row

2a: with Col-B make slip knot on hook, draw slip knot through first loop on hook (this makes the first stitch of next row).

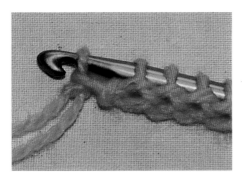

2b: *YO and draw through next 2 loops on hook (one loop of each colour), repeat from * across, leaving last loop on hook (this loop counts as first vertical bar of next row), do not turn (the stitches on this row are called horizontal bars).

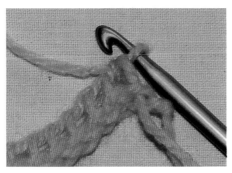

Row 3: Pick-up row: cont. with Col-B, *insert hook under next vertical bar and draw up a loop, leave loop on hook, repeat from * across, drop Col-B, turn hook and slide all loops to opposite end of hook.

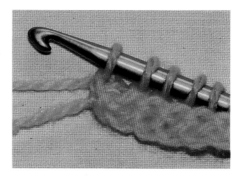

Row 4: Cast-off row: pick up Col-A from row below and draw through one loop (first stitch of next row), then continue as in cast-off row 2b.

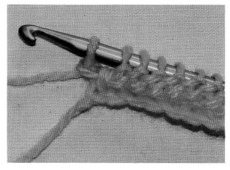

Row 5: Pick-up row: cont. with col-A, *insert hook under next vertical bar and draw up a loop, leave loop on hook, repeat from * across, drop Col-A, turn hook and slide all loops to opposite end of hook.

Row 6: Cast-off row: pick up Col-B from row below and draw through one loop (first stitch of next row) then continue as in cast-off row 2b.

Repeat Rows 3 to 6 to desired size, ending with Row 4 and finishing with a last row of ss under in each vertical bar across, finish off.

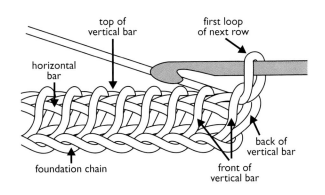

top of
vertical bar

first loop
of next row

horizontal
bar

foundation chain

back of
vertical bar

front of
vertical bar

Round 2: ch 1, dc (US sc) in same st, *3 dc (US sc) in next corner st, dc (US sc) in each st across to next corner st, repeat from * around, join with ss in first dc (US sc), finish off — 132 dc (US sc).

MARKERS

Use markers for easy identification of top/bottom of work and corner stitches in edging.

Last row: unless otherwise stated in pattern, always make 1 ch, then ss or dc (US sc) into each vertical or horizontal bar as directed in pattern.

ABBREVIATIONS

ch	chain
ss	slip stitch
dc (US sc)	double crochet
	(US single crochet)
tr (US dc)	treble (US double crochet)
st	stitch
lp/lps	loop/loops
dec	decrease
dtr (US tr)	double treble (US treble)
BPtr (US BPdc)	Back Post treble
	(US Back Post double crochet)
FPtr (US FPdc)	Front Post treble
	(US Front Post double crochet)
YO	yarn over
sp	space
opp	opposite
cont.	continue

EDGING FOR INDIVIDUAL SQUARES

Use ordinary crochet hook for edging. I recommend that as you complete each square according to the instructions, you finish it with these two rounds of edging. If you don't edge as you go you will end up with a pile of 30 squares needing to be done one after the other—very tedious.

Round 1: with Col-A side facing, join Col-C with dc (US sc) in first st of last row, work 2 dc (US sc) in same st, then work 28 dc (US sc) evenly across each side with 3 dc (US sc) in each corner st around, join with ss to first dc (US sc), do not finish off — 124 dc (US sc).

CROCHENIT DIAGRAM SYMBOLS

○ chain/ch

●○○○○○○○○ foundation ch

◀ finish off

↪ turn

~ yarn over/YO

— return st

● slip stitch/ss

● slip loop/S-lp

✕ double crochet/dc (US single crochet/sc)

╎ double crochet loop/dc lp
(US single crochet loop/sc lp)

† half treble loop/htr lp (US half double
crochet loop/hdc lp)

╪ treble loop/tr lp (US double crochet
loop/dc lp)

╪ Short treble loop/Str lp (US short
double crochet loop/Sdc lp)

╱╱ double treble loop/dtr lp (US treble loop/tr lp)

╎ loop under vertical bar/knit st

╎ loop under horizontal bar

ⱴⱴ loop in space

╎ loop in ch on top of vertical bar

╎ loop under vertical and horizontal bar

⌐ loop under 2 vertical bars

⌐ loop under 2 horizontal bars

⟨ ⟩ row

↑↑↑↑↑↑ last row in dc (US sc)

┬┬┬┬┬┬ last row in ss

⋀ ⋀ decrease
a   b

╱ slant stitch

◗◗◗ puff stitch
a b c

⌐ simple shell st

⌐ chenille stitch

⌐ twisted knit stitch

✕ cross stitch

✕ high cross stitch

⌐⌐⌐⌐ spike or long stitch
a b c d

◊◊ clusters
a   b

Front Post double treble loop/
FPdtr lp (US FPtr lp); FPtr lp
(US FPdc lp); FPdc lp
(US FPsc lp)
a b c d e f

Back Post double treble loop/
BPdtr lp (US BPtr lp); BPtr lp
(US BPdc lp); BPdc lp
(US BPsc lp)
a b c d e f

∜ birdsfoot stitch

limpet or winding stitch

twisted cable
a   b

use back bar of chain
skip
circlet stitch

circlet st detail

SQUARE 1: BASIC KNIT STITCH

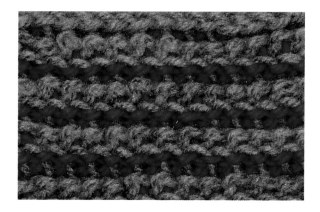
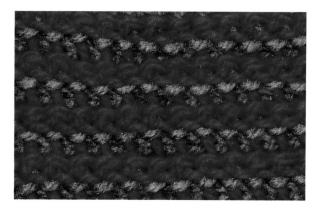

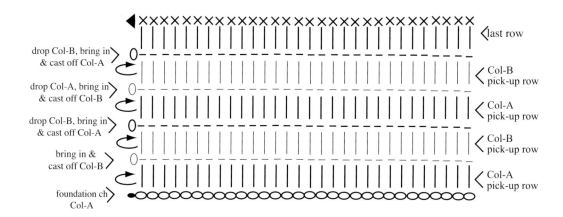

Foundation row: make 30 ch.

Row 1 and subsequent rows: follow directions for basic two-colour crochenit technique on page 158 to desired size.

SQUARE 2: HORIZONTAL KNIT STITCH

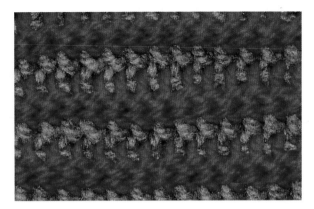

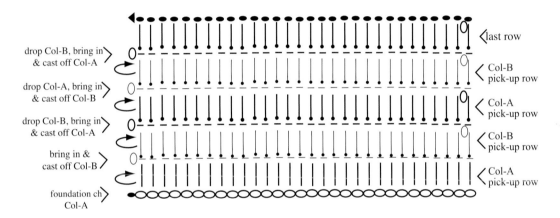

Foundation row: with col-A make 30 ch.

Row 1: cont. with Col-A draw up a loop in 2nd ch from hook and in each ch across, drop Col-A, turn, slide loops to opp end of hook.

Row 2: with Col-B make slip knot onto hook and cast off as for basic crochenit Row 2 until one loop remains; do not turn.

Row 3: cont. with Col-B make 1 ch, *insert hook under next horizontal bar and draw up a loop, repeat from * across, drop Col-B, turn, slide loops to opp end of hook.

Row 4: pick up Col-A from row below and cast off until one loop remains; do not turn.

Row 5: cont. with Col-A make 1 ch, *insert hook under next horizontal bar and draw up a loop, repeat from * across, drop Col-A, turn, slide loops to opp end of hook.

Row 6: pick up Col-B from row below and cast off until one loop remains; do not turn.

Row 7: cont. with Col-B make 1 ch, *insert hook under next horizontal bar and draw up a loop, repeat from * across, drop Col-B, turn, slide lps to opp end of hook.

Repeat Rows 4 to 7 to desired size, ending with Row 4 and finishing with a last row of ss in horizontal bars across; finish off.

SQUARE 3: WAFFLE STITCH

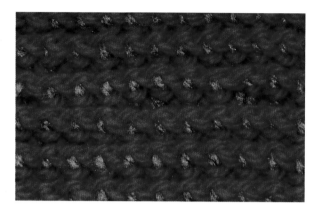

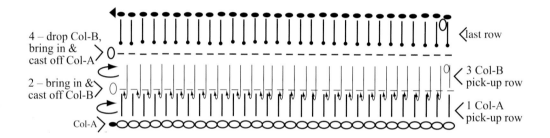

Foundation row: with col-A make 30 ch.

Row 1: cont. with Col-A draw up a loop in 2nd ch from hook and in each ch across, drop Col-A, turn, slide loops to opp end of hook — 30 lps.

Row 2: with Col-B make slip knot onto hook and cast off as for basic crochenit Row 2 until one loop remains; do not turn.

Row 3: cont. with Col-B make 1 ch, *insert hook in sp under next horizontal bar and draw up a loop, repeat from * across, drop Col-B, turn, slide loops to opp end of hook.

Row 4: pick up Col-A from row below and cast off until one loop remains; do not turn.

Row 5: cont. with Col-A make 1 ch, *insert hook in sp under next horizontal bar, YO and draw up a loop, repeat from * across, drop Col-A, turn, slide loops to opp end of hook.

Row 6: pick up Col-B from row below and cast off until one loop remains; do not turn.

Row 7: cont. with Col-B repeat Row 3.

Repeat Rows 4 to 7 to desired size, ending with Row 4 and finishing with a last row of ss under each horizontal bars across; finish off.

SQUARE 4: DIAGONAL STRIPE

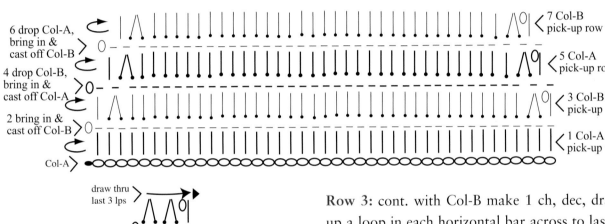

6 drop Col-A, bring in & cast off Col-B
4 drop Col-B, bring in & cast off Col-A
2 bring in & cast off Col-B
Col-A

7 Col-B pick-up row
5 Col-A pick-up row
3 Col-B pick-up row
1 Col-A pick-up row

draw thru last 3 lps

5 lps remain

⋀ **Decrease/dec** insert hook in next 2 horizontal bars at same time, YO and draw through both bars.

FIRST HALF

Foundation row: with col-A make 41 ch.

Row 1: cont. with Col-A draw up a loop in 2nd ch from hook and in each ch across, drop Col-A, turn, slide loops to opp end of hook — 41 lps.

Row 2: with Col-B make slip knot onto hook and cast off as for basic crochenit Row 2 until one loop remains; do not turn.

Row 3: cont. with Col-B make 1 ch, dec, draw up a loop in each horizontal bar across to last 3 horizontal bars, dec, draw up a loop in last horizontal bar, drop Col-B, turn, slide loops to opp end of hook — 39 lps.

Row 4: pick up Col-A from row below and cast off until one loop remains; do not turn.

Row 5: cont. with Col-A make 1 ch, dec, draw up a loop in each horizontal bar across to last 3 horizontal bars, dec, draw up a loop in last horizontal bar, drop Col-A, turn, slide loops to opp end of hook — 37 lps.

Row 6: pick up Col-B from row below and cast off until one loop remains; do not turn.

Row 7: cont. with Col-B repeat Row 3 — 35 lps.

Repeat Rows 4 to 7 until 5 loops remain, dec twice, turn, with col-A draw through 3 loops; finish off.

SECOND HALF

With Col-B facing, foundation ch at top and starting ch on right, join Col-A with ss in starting ch, then draw up a loop in each ch across — 41 lps.

Repeat from Row 2 of first half until 5 loops remain, dec twice, turn, with col-A draw through 3 loops; finish off.

SQUARE 5: EASY CROCHENIT RIB STITCH

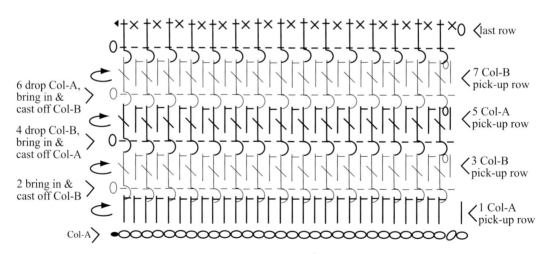

⌐ Double crochet loop/dc lp (US single crochet loop/sc lp)

insert hook in next ch or st and draw up a loop, YO and draw through one loop on hook.

↟ Front Post half treble/FPhtr (US Front Post half double crochet/FPhdc)

YO, insert hook from right to left around both strands of next vertical bar and draw up a loop, YO and draw through 3 loops.

Front Post treble loop/FPtr lp (US Front Post double crochet loop/FPdc lp)

YO, insert hook from right to left around both strands of next vertical bar and draw up a loop, YO and draw through 2 loops.

Foundation row: with col-A make 31 ch.

Row 1: cont. with Col-A draw up a loop in 3rd ch from hook, dc lp (US sc lp) in each ch across, drop Col-A, turn, slide loops to opp end of hook — 30 lps from now on.

Row 2: with Col-B make slip knot onto hook and cast off as for basic crochenit Row 2 until one loop remains; do not turn.

Row 3: cont. with Col-B make 1 ch, *work FPtr lp (US FPdc lp) around next vertical bar, work dc lp (US sc lp) in next vertical bar, repeat from * across, drop Col-B, turn, slide loops to opp end of hook.

Row 4: pick up Col-A from row below and cast off until one loop remains; do not turn.

Row 5: cont. with Col-A make 1 ch, *work FPtr lp (US FPdc lp) around next vertical bar, work dc lp (US sc lp) in next vertical bar, repeat from * across, drop Col-A, turn, slide loops to opp end of hook.

Row 6: pick up Col-B from row below and cast off until one loop remains; do not turn.

Row 7: cont. with Col-B repeat Row 3.

Repeat Rows 4 to 7 to desired size, ending with Row 4 and finishing with a last row as follows: 1 ch, *dc (US sc) in first vertical bar, FPhtr (US FPhdc) around next vertical bar, repeat from * across, finish off.

SQUARE 6: CABLE SHELLS

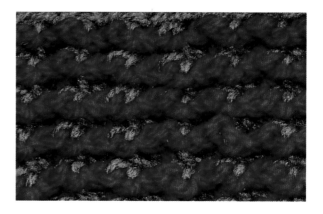

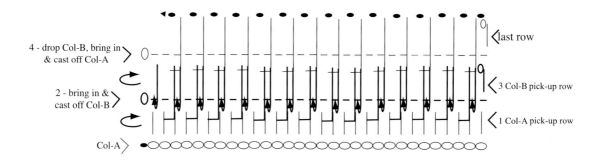

Cable shell: draw up a loop in sp below next horizontal bar, insert hook under next 2 vertical bars, YO and draw through both bars at same time.

Foundation row: with Col-A make 30 ch.

Row 1: cont. with Col-A draw up a loop in 2nd ch from hook and in each ch across, drop Col-A, turn, slide loops to opp end of hook — 30 lps.

Row 2: with Col-B make slip knot onto hook and cast off as for basic crochenit Row 2 until one loop remains; do not turn.

Row 3: cont. with Col-B make 1 ch, work cable shell across to last horizontal bar, draw up a loop in sp under last horizontal bar, drop Col-B, turn, slide loops to opp end of hook — 30 lps.

Row 4: pick up Col-A from row below and cast off until one loop remains; do not turn.

Row 5: cont. with Col-A make 1 ch, work cable shell across to last horizontal bar, draw up a loop in sp under last horizontal bar, drop Col-A, turn, slide loops to opp end of hook — 30 lps.

Row 6: pick up Col-B from row below and cast off until one loop remains; do not turn.

Row 7: cont. with Col-B repeat Row 3 — 30 lps.

Repeat Rows 4 to 7 to desired size, ending with row 4 and finishing with a last row as follows: 1 ch, *ss in sp under next horizontal bar, insert hook in next 2 vertical bars, YO and draw through both bars and loop on hook, repeat from * across; finish off.

SQUARE 7: EASY SHELLS

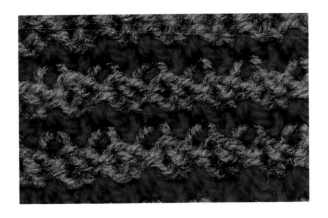
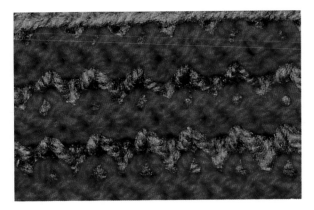

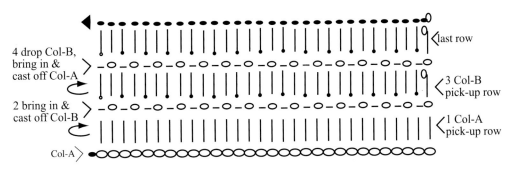

4 drop Col-B, bring in & cast off Col-A

2 bring in & cast off Col-B

Col-A

last row

3 Col-B pick-up row

1 Col-A pick-up row

Foundation row: with col-A make 30 ch.

Row 1: cont. with Col-A draw up a loop in 2nd ch from hook and in each ch across, drop Col-A, turn, slide loops to opp end of hook — 30 lps.

Row 2: with Col-B make slip knot onto hook and draw through first 2 loops (easy shell made), *1 ch, YO and draw through 3 loops, repeat from * across until one loop remains; do not turn.

Row 3: cont. with Col-B make 1 ch, draw up a loop in each horizontal bar and each 1 ch across to last easy shell, draw up a loop in top of last easy shell, drop Col-B, turn, slide loops to opp end of hook.

Row 4: pick up Col-A from row below and draw through first 2 loops (easy shell made), *1 ch,

YO and draw through 3 loops, repeat from * across until one loop remains; do not turn.

Row 5: cont. with Col-A make 1 ch, draw up a loop in each horizontal bar and each 1 ch across to last easy shell, draw up a loop in top of last easy shell, drop Col-A, turn, slide loops to opp end of hook.

Row 6: pick up Col-B from row below and draw through first 2 loops (easy shell made), *1 ch, YO and draw through 3 loops, repeat from * across until one loop remains; do not turn.

Row 7: cont. with Col-B repeat Row 3.

Repeat Rows 4 to 7 to desired size, ending with Row 4 and finishing with a last row of ss in each horizontal bar and 1 ch across to last easy shell, ss in top of last easy shell; finish off.

SQUARE 8: SIMPLE SHELLS

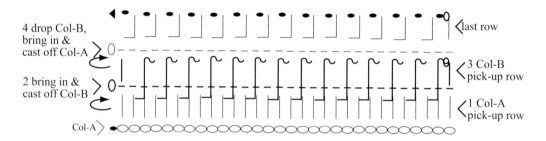

Simple shell stitch: YO, insert hook under next 2 vertical bars, YO and draw loop through both bars.

Foundation row: with col-A make 30 ch.

Row 1: cont. with Col-A draw up a loop in 2nd ch from hook and in each ch across, drop Col-A, turn, slide loops to opp end of hook — 30 lps.

Row 2: with Col-B make slip knot onto hook and cast off as for basic crochenit Row 2 until one loop remains; do not turn.

Row 3: cont. with Col-B make 1 ch, work simple shell stitch across to last vertical bar, draw up a loop in last vertical bar, drop Col-B, turn, slide loops to opp end of hook.

Row 4: pick up Col-A from row below and cast off until one loop remains; do not turn.

Row 5: cont. with Col-A make 1 ch, work simple shell stitch across to last vertical bar, draw up a loop in last vertical bar, drop Col-A, turn, slide loops to opp end of hook.

Row 6: pick up Col-B from row below and cast off until one loop remains; do not turn.

Row 7: cont. with Col-B repeat Row 3.

Repeat Rows 4 to 7 to desired size, ending with Row 4 and finishing with a last row as follows: 1 ch, *ss in next horizontal bar, insert hook in next 2 vertical bars, YO and draw through both bars *and* loop on hook, repeat from * across; finish off.

SQUARE 9: HIGH SHELLS

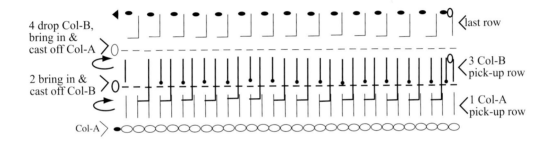

High shell stitch: draw up a loop in next horizontal bar, insert hook under next 2 vertical bars, YO and draw loop through both bars.

Foundation row: with Col-A make 30 ch.

Row 1: cont. with Col-A draw up a loop in 2nd ch from hook and in each ch across, drop Col-A, turn, slide loops to opp end of hook — 30 lps.

Row 2: with Col-B make slip knot onto hook and cast off as for basic crochenit Row 2 until one loop remains; do not turn.

Row 3: cont. with Col-B make 1 ch, work high shell stitch across to last horizontal bar, draw up a loop in last horizontal bar, drop Col-B, turn, slide loops to opp end of hook.

Row 4: pick up Col-A from row below and cast off until one loop remains; do not turn.

Row 5: cont. with Col-A make 1 ch, work high shell stitch across to last horizontal bar, draw up a loop in last horizontal bar, drop Col-A, turn, slide loops to opp end of hook.

Row 6: pick up Col-B from row below and cast off until one loop remains; do not turn.

Row 7: cont. with Col-B repeat Row 3.

Repeat Rows 4 to 7 to desired size, ending with Row 4 and finishing with a last row as follows: 1 ch, *ss in next horizontal bar, insert hook in next 2 vertical bars, YO and draw through both bars and loop on hook, repeat from * across; finish off.

SQUARE 10: RELIEF SHELLS

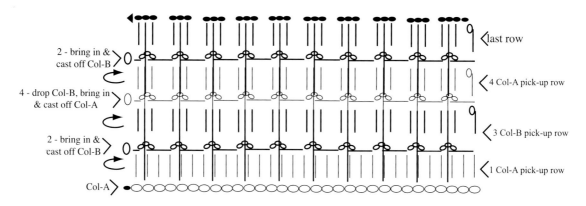

Foundation row: with col-A make 31 ch.

Row 1: cont. with Col-A draw up a loop in 2nd ch from hook and in each ch across, drop Col-A, turn, slide loops to opp end of hook — 31 lps.

Row 2: with Col-B make slip knot onto hook and draw through one loop, *2 ch, YO and draw through 4 loops (counts as 3 ch and one shell), repeat from * until one loop remains; do not turn.

Row 3: cont. with Col-B make 1 ch, *skip next shell, draw up loop in first ch of next 3 ch, insert hook in ch directly below on Row 1, YO and draw up a loop, draw up loop in 3rd ch of same 3 ch just worked, repeat from * across to end, drop Col-B, turn, slide loops to opp end of hook — 31 lps.

Row 4: pick up Col-A from row below and draw through one loop, *2 ch, YO and draw through 4 loops, repeat from * until one loop remains; do not turn.

Row 5: cont. with Col-A make 1 ch, * skip next shell, draw up loop in first ch of next 3 ch, insert hook in ch on row directly below, YO and draw up a loop, draw up loop in 3rd ch of same 3 ch just worked, repeat from * across to end, drop Col-A, turn, slide loops to opp end of hook — 31 lps.

Row 6: pick up Col-B from row below and draw through one loop, *2 ch, YO and draw through 4 loops, repeat from * until one loop remains; do not turn.

Row 7: cont. with Col-B repeat Row 3 — 31 lps.

Repeat Rows 4 to 7 to desired size, ending with Row 4 and finishing with a last row as follows: ss in first ch of next 3 ch, ss in ch on row directly below and ss in 3rd ch of same 3 ch just worked, repeat across; finish off. Refer to diagram.

SQUARE 11: CROSS STITCH

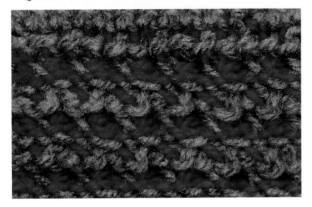
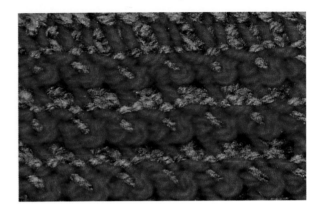

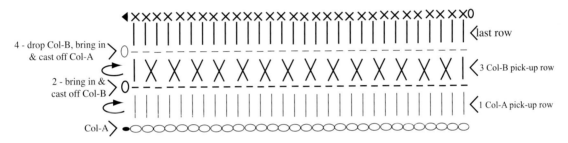

Y **Cross stitch:** skip next vertical bar, draw up a loop in next vertical bar, draw up a loop in skipped vertical bar.

Foundation row: with col-A make 30 ch.

Row 1: cont. with Col-A draw up a loop in 2nd ch from hook and in each ch across, drop Col-A, turn, slide loops to opp end of hook — 30 lps.

Row 2: with Col-B make slip knot onto hook and cast off as for basic crochenit Row 2 until one loop remains; do not turn.

Row 3: cont. with Col-B, work cross stitch across to last vertical bar, draw up a loop in last vertical bar, drop Col-B, turn, slide loops to opp end of hook.

Row 4: pick up Col-A from row below and cast off until one loop remains; do not turn.

Row 5: cont. with Col-A, work cross stitch across to last vertical bar, draw up a loop in last vertical bar, drop Col-A, turn, slide loops to opp end of hook.

Row 6: pick up Col-B from row below and cast off until one loop remains; do not turn.

Row 7: cont. with Col-B repeat Row 3.

Repeat Rows 4 to 7 to desired size, ending with Row 4 and finishing with a last row of dc (US sc) in each vertical bar across; finish off.

SQUARE 12: HIGH CROSS STITCH

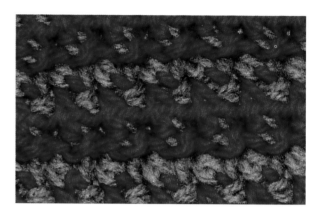

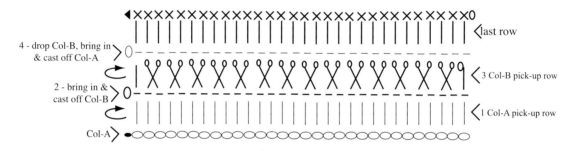

High cross stitch: skip next vertical bar, draw up a loop in next vertical bar, 1 ch in loop just made, draw up a loop in skipped vertical bar, 1 ch in loop just made.

Foundation row: with col-A make 30 ch.

Row 1: cont. with Col-A draw up a loop in 2nd ch from hook and in each ch across, drop Col-A, turn, slide loops to opp end of hook — 30 lps.

Row 2: with Col-B make slip knot onto hook and cast off as for basic crochenit Row 2 until one loop remains; do not turn.

Row 3: cont. with Col-B make 1 ch, work high cross stitch across to last vertical bar, draw up a loop in last vertical bar, 1 ch in last loop, drop Col-B, turn, slide loops to opp end of hook.

Row 4: pick up Col-A from row below and cast off until one loop remains; do not turn.

Row 5: cont. with Col-A make 1 ch, work high cross stitch across to last vertical bar, draw up a loop in last vertical bar, 1 ch in last loop, drop Col-A, turn, slide loops to opp end of hook.

Row 6: pick up Col-B from row below and cast off until one loop remains; do not turn.

Row 7: cont. with Col-B repeat Row 3.

Repeat Rows 4 to 7 to desired size, ending with row 4 and finishing with a last row of dc (US sc) in each vertical bar across; finish off.

SQUARE 13: RELIEF POST STITCH NO. 1

 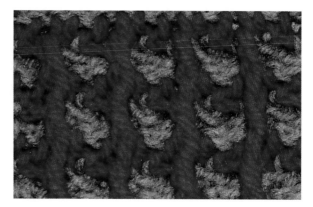

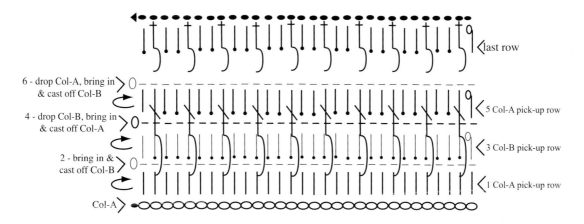

6 - drop Col-A, bring in & cast off Col-B

4 - drop Col-B, bring in & cast off Col-A

2 - bring in & cast off Col-B

Col-A

last row
5 Col-A pick-up row
3 Col-B pick-up row
1 Col-A pick-up row

Front Post treble loop/FPtr lp (US Front Post double crochet loop/FPdc lp)

YO, insert hook from right to left around both strands of vertical bar indicated, YO and draw through one loop, YO and draw through 2 loops.

Front Post half treble/FPhtr (US Front Post half double crochet/FPhdc)

YO, insert hook from right to left around both strands of next vertical bar, YO and draw through a loop, YO and draw through 3 loops.

Foundation row: with col-A make 30 ch.

Row 1: cont. with Col-A draw up a loop in 2nd ch from hook and in each ch across, drop Col-A, turn, slide loops to opp end of hook — 30 lps.

Row 2: with Col-B make slip knot onto hook and cast off as for basic crochenit Row 2 until one loop remains; do not turn.

Row 3: cont. with Col-B make 1 ch, draw up loop in next horizontal bar, and in each horizontal bar across, drop Col-B, turn, slide loops to opp end of hoo.

Row 4: pick up Col-A from row below and cast off until one loop remains; do not turn.

Row 5: cont. with Col-A make 1 ch, *FPtr lp (US FPdc lp) around vertical bar directly 4 rows below, draw up loop in next 2 horizontal bars, repeat from * across to last horizontal bar, draw up loop in last horizontal bar, drop Col-A, turn, slide loops to opp end of hook.

Row 6: pick up Col-B from row below and cast off until one loop remains; do not turn.

Row 7: cont. with Col-B make 1 ch, *FPtr lp (US FPdc lp) around vertical bar directly 4 rows below, draw up loop in next 2 horizontal bars, repeat from * across to last horizontal bar, draw up a loop in last horizontal bar, drop Col-B, turn, slide loops to opp end of hook.

Row 8: repeat Row 4.

Repeat Rows 5 to 8 to desired size, ending with row 4 and finishing with a last row as follows: 1 ch, *FPhtr (US FPhdc) around vertical bar directly 4 rows below, ss in next 2 horizontal bars, repeat from * across, ss in last horizontal bar; finish off.

SQUARE 14: RELIEF POST STITCH NO. 2

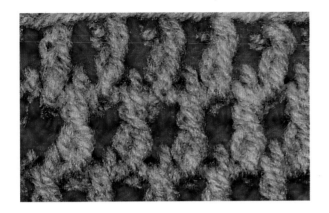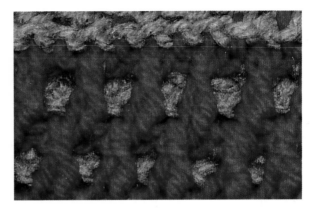

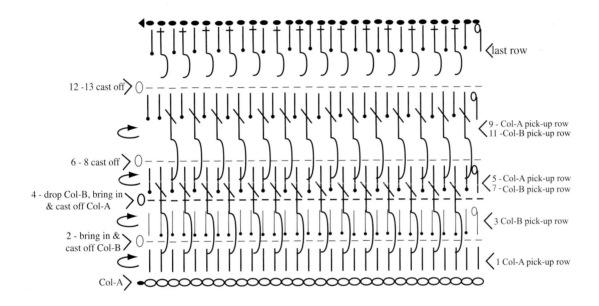

Front Post treble loop/FPtr lp (US Front Post double crochet loop/FPdc lp)

YO, insert hook from right to left around both strands of vertical bar indicated, YO and draw through one loop, YO and draw through 2 loops

Front Post half treble/FPhtr (US Front Post half double crochet/FPhdc)

YO, insert hook from right to left around both strands of next vertical bar, YO and draw through a loop, YO and draw through 3 loops

Foundation row: with col-A make 30 ch.

Row 1: cont. with Col-A draw up a loop in 2nd ch from hook and in each ch across, drop Col-A, turn, slide loops to opp end of hook — 30 lps.

Row 2: with Col-B make slip knot onto hook and cast off as for basic crochenit Row 2 until one loop remains; do not turn.

Row 3: cont. with Col-B make 1 ch, draw up loop in next horizontal bar, and in each horizontal bar across, drop Col-B, turn, slide loops to opp end of hook.

Row 4: pick up Col-A from row below and cast off until one loop remains; do not turn.

Row 5: cont. with Col-A make 1 ch, draw up a loop in next horizontal bar, *FPtr lp (US FPdc lp) around vertical bar directly 4 rows below, draw up loop in next horizontal bar, repeat from * across to last horizontal bar, draw up loop in last horizontal bar, drop Col-A, turn, slide loops to opp end of hook.

Row 6: pick up Col-B from row below and cast off until one loop remains; do not turn.

Row 7: cont. with Col-B repeat Row 5, drop Col-B, turn, slide loops to opp end of hook.

Row 8: repeat Row 4.

Row 9: cont. with Col-A make 1 ch, *FPtr lp (US FPdc lp) around vertical bar directly 4 rows below, draw up loop in next horizontal bar, repeat from * across to last 2 horizontal bars, draw up loop in last 2 horizontal bars, drop Col-A, turn, slide loops to opp end of hook.

Row 10: repeat Row 6.

Row 11: cont. with Col-B repeat Row 9.

Repeat Rows 4 to 11 to desired size, ending with Row 4 and finishing with a last row as follows: 1 ch, *ss in next horizontal bar, FPhtr (US FPhdc) around both strands of next vertical bar 4 rows below, repeat from * across; finish off.

SQUARE 15: CROCHENIT AND BIRDSFOOT STITCH

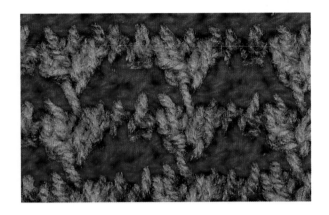
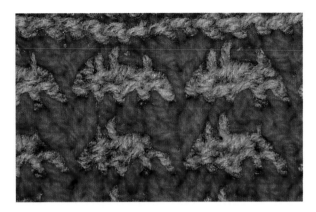

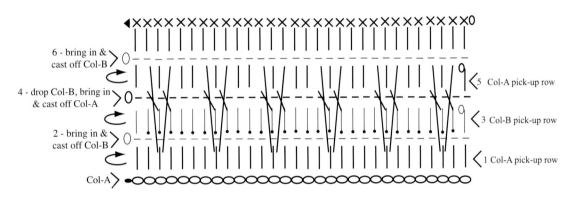

6 - bring in & cast off Col-B

4 - drop Col-B, bring in & cast off Col-A

2 - bring in & cast off Col-B

Col-A

5 Col-A pick-up row

3 Col-B pick-up row

1 Col-A pick-up row

Treble loop/tr lp (US double crochet loop/dc lp)

YO, insert hook under vertical bar indicated and draw up a loop, YO and draw through one loop, YO and draw through 2 loops.

Birdsfoot stitch: work 2 tr lps (US dc lps) as follows:

first tr lp (US dc lp): work tr lp (US dc lp) under vertical bar 4 rows below and one st forward, 1 loop in next horizontal bar;

second tr lp (US dc lp): work under same vertical bar on 4th row as in first tr lp (US dc lp).

Foundation row: with Col-A make 30 ch.

Row 1: cont. with Col-A draw up a loop in 2nd ch from hook and in each ch across, drop Col-A, turn, slide loops to opp end of hook — 30 lps.

Row 2: with Col-B make slip knot onto hook and cast off as for basic crochenit Row 2 until one loop remains; do not turn.

Row 3: cont. with Col-B make 1 ch, draw up loop in next horizontal bar, and in each horizontal bar across, drop Col-B, turn, slide loops to opp end of hook.

Row 4: pick up Col-A from row below and cast off until one loop remains; do not turn.

Row 5: cont. with Col-A make 1 ch, *work birdsfoot st, draw up loop in next 2 horizontal bars, repeat from * across to last horizontal bar, draw up loop in last horizontal bar, drop Col-A, turn, slide loops to opp end of hook.

Row 6: pick up Col-B from row below and cast off until one loop remains; do not turn.

Row 7: cont. with Col-B make 1 ch, *work birdsfoot st, draw up loop in next 2 horizontal bars, repeat from * across to last horizontal bar, draw up a loop in last horizontal bar, drop Col-B, turn, slide loops to opp end of hook.

Row 8: repeat Row 4.

Repeat Rows 5 to 8 to desired size, ending with Row 4 and finishing with a last row of dc (US sc) in each vertical bar across; finish off.

SQUARE 16: CROCHENIT RIPPLE-WAVE STITCH

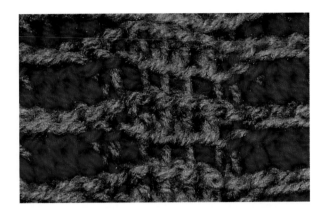
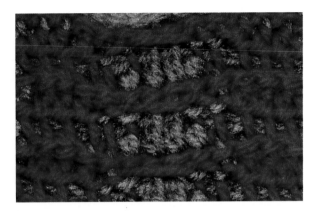

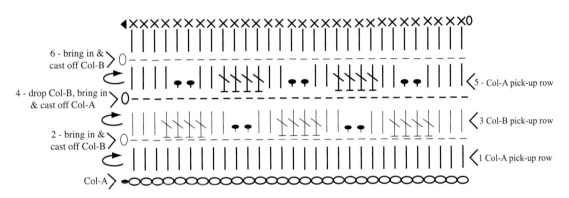

Short treble loop/Str lp (US Short double crochet loop/Sdc lp) YO, insert into next vertical bar and draw up a loop, YO and draw through 2 loops.

Slip loop (S-lp) pick up vertical bar but do not draw through a loop.

Refer to pattern diagram below for easy stitch placement for each colour.

Foundation row: with col-A make 30 ch.

Row 1: cont. with Col-A draw up a loop in 2nd ch from hook and in each ch across, drop Col-A, turn, slide loops to opp end of hook — 30 lps.

Row 2: with Col-B make slip knot onto hook and cast off as for basic crochenit Row 2 until one loop remains; do not turn.

Row 3: cont. with Col-B, draw up a loop in next 2 vertical bars (3 lps on hook), *Str lp (US Sdc lp) in next 4 vertical bars, draw up a loop in next 2 vertical bars, S-lp in next 2 vertical bars, draw up a loop in next 2 vertical bars, repeat from * to last 3 vertical bars, draw up a loop in last 3 vertical bars, drop Col-B, turn, slide loops to opp end of hook.

Row 4: pick up Col-A from row below and cast off until one loop remains; do not turn.

Row 5: cont. with Col-A, draw up a loop in next 3 vertical bars (4 lps on hook), *S-lp in next 2 vertical bars, draw up a loop in next 2 vertical bars, Str lp (US Sdc lp) in next 4 vertical bars, draw up a loop in next 2 vertical bars, repeat from * to last 4 vertical bars, draw up a loop in last 4 vertical bars, drop Col-A, turn, slide loops to opp end of hook.

Row 6: pick up Col-B from row below and cast off until one loop remains; do not turn.

Row 7: cont. with Col-B repeat Row 3.

Repeat Rows 4 to 7 to desired size, ending with Row 4 and finishing with a last row of dc (US sc) under each vertical bar across; finish off.

SQUARE 17: CROCHENIT POPCORNS

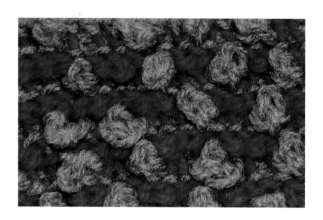

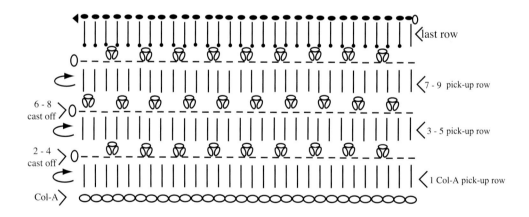

| Loop in horizontal bar

Refer to pattern diagram below for easy stitch placement for each colour.

Foundation row: with col-A make 30 ch.

Row 1: cont. with Col-A draw up a loop in 2nd ch from hook and in each ch across, drop Col-A, turn, slide loops to opp end of hook — 30 lps.

Row 2: with Col-B make slip knot onto hook and cast off as for basic crochenit Row 2 under next 2 loops (3 vertical bars made), *3 ch, (YO, draw through 2 loops on hook) 3 times, repeat from * across; do not turn.

Row 3: *(keep 3ch loop to front of work) cont. with Col-B, draw up a loop in each vertical bar across, drop Col-B, turn, slide loops to opp end of hook

Row 4: pick up Col-A from row below and draw through one loop, cast off next 2 loops *3 ch, (YO, draw through 2 loops on hook) 3 times, repeat from * across; do not turn.

Row 5: cont. with Col-A draw up loops as in Row 3, drop Col-A, turn, slide loops to opp end of hook.

Row 6: pick up Col-B from row below and draw through one loop, *3 ch, (YO, draw through 2 loops on hook) 3 times, repeat from * across to last 2 loops, draw through each of last 2 loops; do not turn.

Row 7: cont. with Col-B draw up loops as in Row 3, drop Col-B, turn, slide loops to opp end of hook.

Row 8: pick up Col-A from row below and cast off as in Row 6; do not turn.

Row 9: cont. with Col-A draw up loops as in Row 3, drop Col-A, turn, slide loops to opp end of hook.

Repeat Rows 2 to 9 to desired size, ending with Row 4 and finishing with a last row of ss under each horizontal bar across; finish off.

SQUARE 18: PUFF STITCH

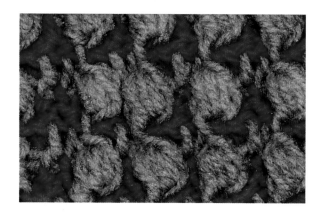

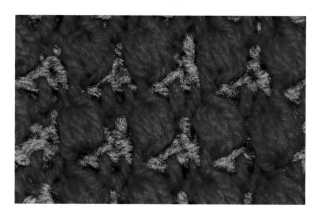

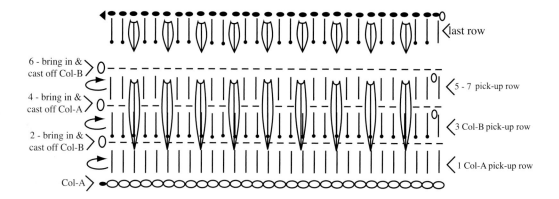

Puff stitch/puff st: YO, draw up a loop in next vertical bar of same col 4 rows below, (YO and draw up a loop in same bar) 2 times more, YO and draw through 6 loops on hook, 1 ch.

Last row puff st: work puff as above until 2 loops remain, draw 1 ch loop through ss loop.

Loop in horizontal bar

Refer to pattern diagram below for easy stitch placement.

Foundation row: with col-A make 30 ch.

Row 1: cont. with Col-A draw up a loop in 2nd ch from hook and in each ch across, drop Col-A, turn, slide loops to opp end of hook — 30 lps.

Row 2: with Col-B make slip knot onto hook and cast off as for basic crochenit Row 2 until one loop remains; do not turn.

Row 3: cont. with Col-B make 1 ch, draw up a loop in next horizontal bar and in each horizontal bar across, drop Col-B, turn, slide loops to opp end of hook.

Row 4: pick up Col-A from row below and cast off until one loop remains; do not turn.

Row 5: cont. with Col-A make 1 ch, draw up a loop in next 2 horizontal bars (3 loops on hook), *work puff st, draw up a loop in next 2 horizontal bars, repeat from * across, drop Col-A, turn, slide loops to opp end of hook.

Row 6: pick up Col-B from row below and cast off until one loop remains; do not turn.

Row 7: cont. with Col-B make 1 ch, draw up a loop in next 2 horizontal bars, *work puff st, draw up a loop in next 2 horizontal bars, repeat from * across, drop Col-B, turn, slide loops to opp end of hook — 30 lps.

Repeat Rows 4 to 7 to desired size, ending with Row 4 and finishing with a last row as follows: 1 ch, ss under next 2 horizontal bars, *work last row puff st, ss under next 2 horizontal bars, repeat from * across; finish off.

SQUARE 19: STAGGERED CLUSTERS

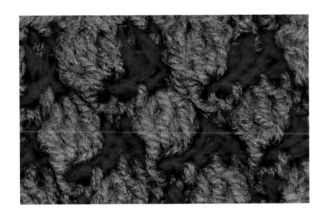
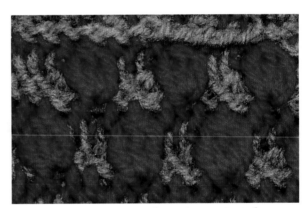

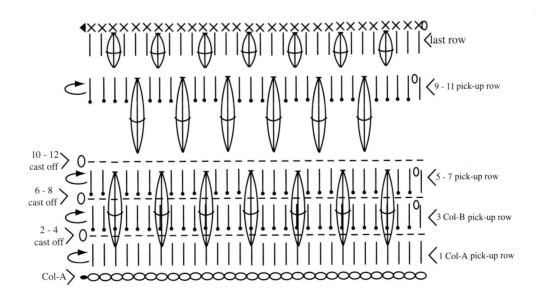

Treble loop/tr lp (US double crochet loop/dc lp)

YO, insert hook under vertical bar indicated and draw up a loop, YO and draw through one loop, YO and draw through 2 loops.

 Treble cluster stitch/tr cluster st (US double crochet cluster stitch/dc cluster st)

Working in vertical bar directly 4 rows below, work 3 tr lp (US dc lp) in vertical bar indicated, YO and draw through 3 loops on hook.

Last row treble cluster stitch (US last row double crochet cluster st)

work tr cluster st (US double crochet cluster st) as above until 2 loops remain, YO and draw through both cluster loop and dc (US sc).

Refer to pattern diagram below for easy stitch placement.

Foundation row: with col-A make 30 ch.

Row 1: cont. with Col-A draw up a loop in 2nd ch from hook and in each ch across, drop Col-A, turn, slide loops to opp end of hook — 30 lps.

Row 2: with Col-B make slip knot onto hook and cast off as for basic crochenit Row 2 until one loop remains; do not turn.

Row 3: cont. with Col-B make 1 ch, draw up a loop in next horizontal bar and in each horizontal bar across, drop Col-B, turn, slide loops to opp end of hook.

Row 4: pick up Col-A from row below and cast off until one loop remains; do not turn.

Row 5: cont. with Col-A make 1 ch, draw up a loop in next 2 horizontal bars (3 loops on hook), *work tr cluster st (US dc cluster st), draw up a loop in next 3 horizontal bars, repeat from * across to last 2 horizontal bars, draw up a loop in last 2 horizontal bars, drop Col-A, turn, slide loops to opp end of hook.

Row 6: pick up Col-B from row below and cast off until one loop remains; do not turn.

Row 7: cont. with Col-B repeat Row 5, drop Col-B, turn, slide loops to opp end of hook.

Row 8: repeat Row 4.

Row 9: cont. with Col-A make 1 ch, draw up a loop in next 4 horizontal bars (5 loops on hook), *work tr cluster st (US dc cluster st), draw up a loop in next 3 horizontal bars, repeat from * across to last 4 horizontal bars, draw up a loop in last 4 horizontal bars, drop Col-A, turn, slide loops to opp end of hook.

Row 10: Repeat Row 6.

Row 11: cont. with Col-B repeat Row 9.

Repeat Rows 4 to 11 to desired size, ending with Row 4 and finishing with a last row as follows: 1 ch, work dc (US sc) and last row cluster (US last row dc cluster) in each vertical bar as required across; finish off.

SQUARE 20: DIAGONAL LOOPS AND CLUSTERS

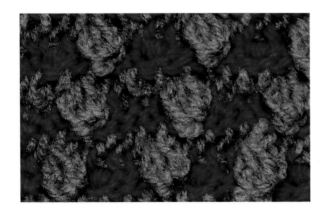
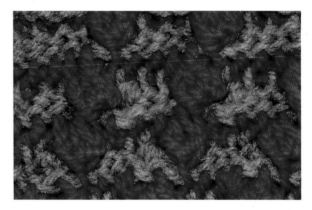

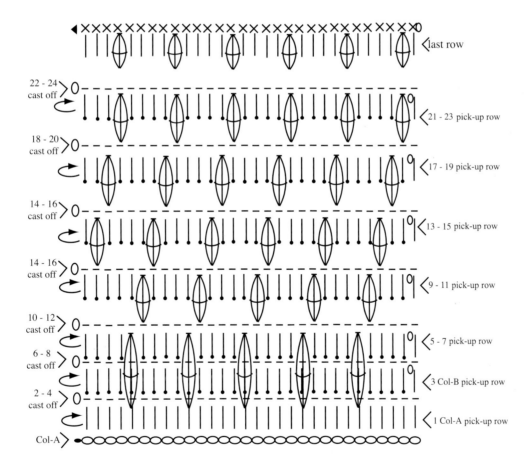

Double crochet loop/dc lp (US Single crochet loop/sc lp)

insert hook in next ch or st and draw up a loop, YO and draw through one loop on hook.

Double crochet cluster stitch/dc cluster st (US single crochet cluster stitch/sc cluster st)

work 3 dc lps in vertical bar directly 4 rows below, YO and draw through 3 loops on hook.

Last row double crochet cluster stitch (US last row single crochet cluster stitch)

work dc cluster st (US single crochet cluster st) as above until 2 loops remain, YO and draw through both loops.

Refer to pattern diagram below for easy stitch placement.

Foundation row: with col-A make 30 ch.

Row 1: cont. with Col-A draw up a loop in 2nd ch from hook and in each ch across, drop Col-A, turn, slide loops to opp end of hook — 30 lps.

Row 2: with Col-B make slip knot onto hook and cast off as for basic crochenit Row 2 until one loop remains; do not turn.

Row 3: cont. with Col-B make 1 ch, draw up a loop in next horizontal bar and in each horizontal bar across, drop Col-B, turn, slide loops to opp end of hook.

Row 4: pick up Col-A from row below and cast off until one loop remains; do not turn.

Row 5: cont. with Col-A make 1 ch, draw up a loop in next 4 horizontal bars (5 loops on hook), *work dc cluster st (US sc cluster st), draw up a loop in next 4 horizontal bars, repeat from * across to last 4 horizontal bars, draw up a loop in last 4 horizontal bars, drop Col-A, turn, slide loops to opp end of hook.

Row 6: pick up Col-B from row below and cast off until one loop remains; do not turn.

Row 7: cont. with Col-B repeat Row 5, drop Col-B, turn, slide loops to opp end of hook.

Row 8: repeat Row 4.

Row 9: cont. with Col-A make 1 ch, draw up a loop in next 3 horizontal bars (4 loops on hook), *work dc cluster st (US sc cluster st), draw up a loop in next 4 horizontal bars, repeat from * across to last 5 horizontal bars, draw up a loop in last 5 horizontal bars, drop Col-A, turn, slide loops to opp end of hook.

Row 10: Repeat Row 6.

Row 11: cont. with Col-B repeat Row 9.

Row 12: Repeat Row 4.

Row 13: cont. with Col-A make 1 ch, draw up a loop in next 2 horizontal bars (3 loops on hook), *work dc cluster st (US sc cluster st), draw up a loop in next 4 horizontal bars, repeat from * across to last horizontal bar, draw up a loop in last horizontal bar, drop Col-A, turn, slide loops to opp end of hook.

Row 14: repeat Row 6.

Row 15: cont. with Col-B repeat Row 13.

Row 16: repeat Row 4.

Row 17: cont. with Col-A make 1 ch, draw up a loop in next horizontal bar (2 loops on hook), *work dc cluster st (US sc cluster st), draw up a loop in next 4 horizontal bars, repeat from * across to last 2 horizontal bars, draw up a loop in last 2 horizontal bars, drop Col-A, turn, slide loops to opp end of hook.

Row 18: repeat Row 6.

Row 19: cont. with Col-B repeat Row 17.

Row 20: repeat Row 4.

Row 21: cont. with Col-A make 1 ch (one loop on hook), *work dc cluster st (US sc cluster st), draw up a loop in next 4 horizontal bars, repeat from * across to last 3 horizontal bars, draw up a loop in last 3 horizontal bars, drop Col-A, turn, slide loops to opp end of hook.

Row 22: repeat Row 6.

Row 23: cont. with Col-B repeat Row 21.

Repeat Rows 4 to 23 to desired size, ending with Row 4 and finishing with a last row as follows: 1 ch, work dc (US sc) and last row dc cluster (US last row sc cluster) in each vertical bar as required across; finish off.

SQUARE 21: LATTICE STITCH

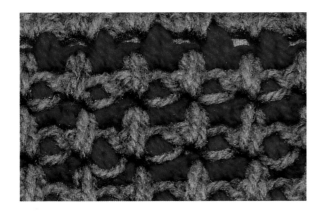
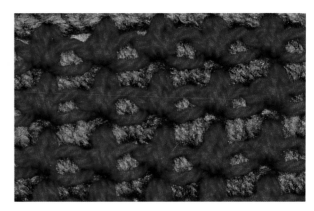

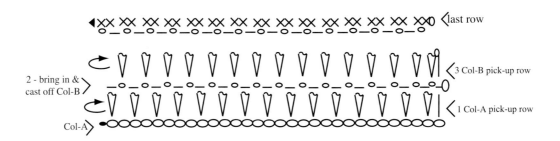

Note: This is a wide pattern—work tightly or use a smaller size hook to stay in line with the other 29 squares.

~ Yarn over hook/YO

Foundation row: with col-A make 30 ch.

Row 1: cont. with Col-A draw up a loop in 2nd ch from hook, YO and draw up a loop on same ch, *skip next ch, draw up a loop in next ch, YO and draw up a loop in same ch, repeat from * across, drop Col-A, turn, slide loops to opp end of hook — 46 lps.

Row 2: with Col-B make slip knot onto hook and draw through one loop, *1 ch, YO and draw through 4 loops on hook, repeat from * across; do not turn — 15 x 1ch sp.

Row 3: cont. with Col-B make 1 ch, *draw up a loop in next 1ch sp, YO and draw up a loop in same sp, repeat from * across, drop Col-B, turn, slide loops to opp end of hook — 46 lps.

Row 4: pick up Col-A from row below and draw through one loop on hook, *1 ch, YO and draw through 4 loops on hook, repeat from * across; do not turn — 15 x 1ch sp.

Row 5: cont. with Col-A make 1 ch, *draw up a loop in next 1-ch sp, YO and draw up a loop in same sp, repeat from * across, drop Col-A, turn, slide loops to opp end of hook — 46 lps.

Row 6: pick up Col-B from row below and draw through one loop on hook, *1 ch, YO and draw through 4 loops on hook, repeat from * across; do not turn — 15 x 1ch sp.

Row 7: cont. with Col-B make 1 ch, *draw up a loop in next 1ch sp, YO and draw up a loop in same sp, repeat from * across, drop Col-A, turn, slide loops to opp end of hook — 46 lps.

Repeat Rows 4 to 7 to desired size, ending with row 4 and finishing with a last row as follows: 1 ch, 2 dc (US sc) into each 1ch sp across; finish off — 30 dc (US sc).

SQUARE 22: CROCHENIT CHENILLE STITCH

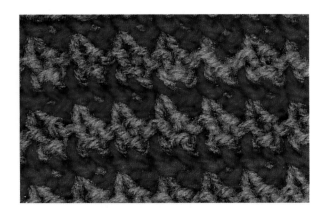 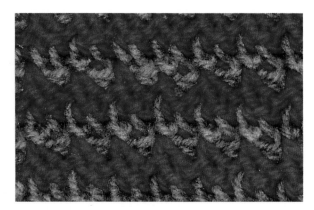

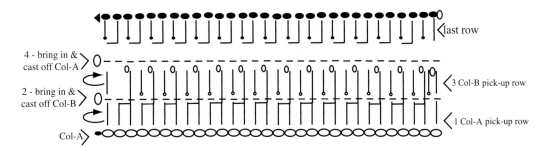

last row

4 - bring in & cast off Col-A

3 Col-B pick-up row

2 - bring in & cast off Col-B

1 Col-A pick-up row

Col-A

Chenille stitch/chenille st

insert hook under next 2 vertical bars, YO and draw up a loop through both bars at the same time, 1 ch through loop just made.

loop in ch on top of vertical bar

Foundation row: with col-A make 30 ch.

Row 1: cont. with Col-A draw up a loop in 2nd ch from hook and in each ch across, drop Col-A, turn, slide loops to opp end of hook — 30 lps.

Row 2: with Col-B make slip knot onto hook and cast off as for basic crochenit Row 2 until one loop remains; do not turn.

Row 3: cont. with Col-B make 1 ch, *draw up a loop in top of next vertical bar, work chenille st, repeat from * across to last vertical bar, draw up a loop in last vertical bar, drop Col-B, turn, slide loops to opp end of hook.

Row 4: pick up Col-A from row below and cast off until one loop remains; do not turn.

Row 5: cont. with Col-A make 1 ch, *draw up a loop in top of next vertical bar, work chenille st, repeat from * across to last vertical bar, draw up a loop in last vertical bar, drop Col-A, turn, slide loops to opp end of hook.

Row 6: pick up Col-B from row below and cast off until one loop remains; do not turn.

Row 7: cont. with Col-B repeat Row 3.

Repeat Rows 4 to 7 to desired size, ending with row 4 and finishing with a last row as follows: 1 ch, *ss in next horizontal bar, insert hook under next 2 vertical bars and draw up a loop through both bars at the same time, draw loop just made through ss, repeat from * across; finish off.

SQUARE 23: TWIST STITCH

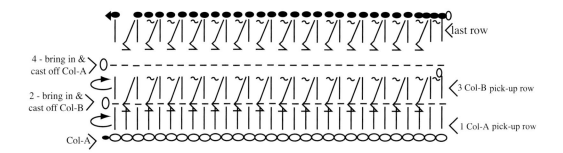

~ Yarn over hook (YO)

⌡ Twist stitch/twist st

with hook sitting over next vertical bar, move hook from left to right, pick up bar while twisting the hook upwards, YO and draw up a loop

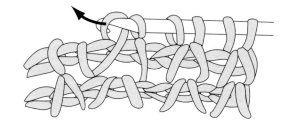

Foundation row: with col-A make 30 ch.

Row 1: cont. with Col-A draw up a loop in 2nd ch from hook and in each ch across, drop Col-A, turn, slide loops to opp end of hook — 30 lps.

Row 2: with Col-B make slip knot onto hook and cast off as for basic crochenit Row 2 until one remains; do not turn.

Row 3: cont. with Col-B make 1 ch, skip first vertical bar, *YO and draw up a loop under next vertical bar, work twist st, YO and draw through 2 loops on hook, repeat from * across to last vertical bar, draw up a loop in last vertical bar, drop Col-B, turn, slide loops to opp end of hook.

Row 4: pick up Col-A from row below and cast off until one loop remains; do not turn.

Row 5: cont. with Col-A make 1 ch, skip first vertical bar, *YO and draw up a loop under next vertical bar, work twist st, YO and draw through 2 loops on hook, repeat from * across to last vertical bar, draw up a loop in last vertical bar, drop Col-A, turn, slide loops to opp end of hook.

Row 6: pick up Col-B from row below and cast off until one loop remains; do not turn.

Row 7: cont. with Col-B repeat Row 3.

Repeat Rows 4 to 7 to desired size, ending with Row 4 and finishing with a last row of ss under each vertical bar and twist st as required across; finish off.

SQUARE 24: LIMPET STITCH

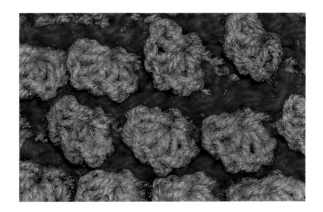

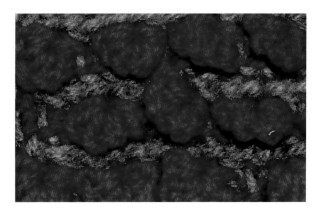

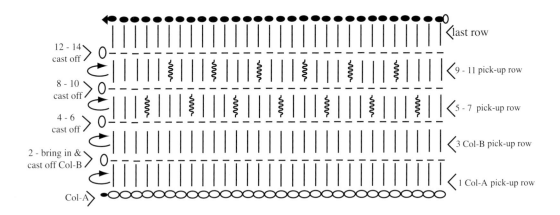

$\rotatebox{-90}{Limpet}$ Limpet stitch/limpet st

insert hook under next vertical bar and cast on 7 new loops as follows: work hook (YO) in an anti-clockwise direction, pick up yarn and draw under and through; do this 7 times (7 extra loops on hook), YO and draw through 8 loops (through the 7 new loops and vertical bar loop), 1 ch to close.

Note: A degree of patience is required for this pattern. Limpet stitches are slow and fiddly to start with but, with a bit of practice, easier than they first appear.

Refer to pattern diagram below for easy stitch placement.

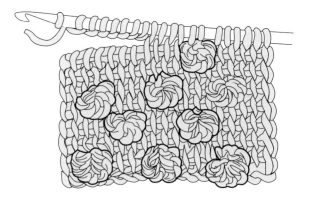

Foundation row: with col-A make 30 ch.

Row 1: cont. with Col-A draw up a loop in 2nd ch from hook and in each ch across, drop Col-A, turn, slide loops to opp end of hook — 30 lps.

Row 2: with Col-B make slip knot onto hook and cast off as for basic crochenit Row 2 until one loop remains; do not turn.

Row 3: cont. with Col-B draw up a loop in each vertical bar across, drop Col-B, turn, slide loops to opp end of hook.

Row 4: pick up Col-A from row below and cast off until one loop remains; do not turn.

Row 5: cont. with Col-A draw up a loop in next vertical bar (2 loops on hook), *work limpet st, draw up a loop in next 3 vertical bars, repeat from * across, drop Col-A, turn, slide loops to opp end of hook.

Row 6: pick up Col-B from row below and cast off until one loop remains; do not turn.

Row 7: cont. with Col-B repeat Row 5.

Row 8: pick up Col-A from row below and cast off until one loop remains; do not turn.

Row 9: cont. with Col-A draw up a loop in next 3 vertical bars (4 loops on hook), *work limpet st, draw up a loop in next 3 vertical bars, repeat from * across to last 5 vertical bars, draw up a loop in last 5 vertical bars, drop Col-A, turn, slide loops to opp end of hook.

Row 10: pick up Col-B from row below and cast off until one loop remains; do not turn.

Row 11: cont. with Col-B repeat Row 9.

Repeat Rows 4 to 11 to desired size, ending with Row 4 and finishing with a last row of ss under each vertical bar across; finish off.

SQUARE 25: SPIKE STITCHES

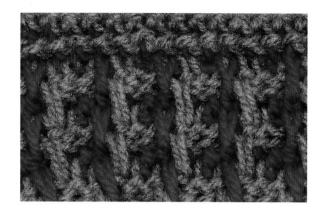
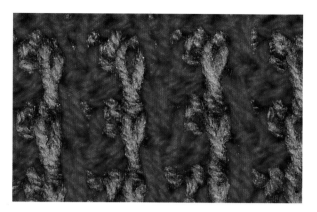

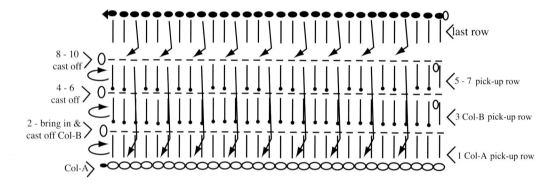

Spike stitch/spike st

insert hook through centre of vertical bar directly 4 rows below, YO and draw up a long loop, 1 ch through loop just made

Last row spike stitch

insert hook through centre of vertical bar directly 4 rows below, YO and draw up a long loop, YO and draw through both loops on hook

Foundation row: with col-A make 30 ch.

Row 1: cont. with Col-A draw up a loop in 2nd ch from hook and in each ch across, drop Col-A, turn, slide loops to opp end of hook — 30 lps.

Row 2: with Col-B make slip knot onto hook and cast off as for basic crochenit Row 2 until one loop remains; do not turn.

Row 3: cont. with Col-B make 1 ch, skip first vertical bar, draw up a loop under each horizontal bar across, drop Col-B, turn, slide loops to opp end of hook.

Row 4: pick up Col-A from row below and cast off until one loop remains; do not turn.

Row 5: cont. with Col-A make 1 ch, skip first vertical bar, draw up a loop under next 2 horizontal bars (3 loops on hook), *work spike st, draw up a loop under next 2 horizontal bars, repeat from * across, drop Col-A, turn, slide loops to opp end of hook.

Row 6: pick up Col-B from row below and cast off until one loop remains; do not turn.

Row 7: cont. with Col-B repeat Row 5.

Repeat Rows 4 to 7 to desired size, ending with Row 4 and finishing with a last row of ss under next 2 vertical bars and last row spike st across; finish off.

SQUARE 26: CROCHENIT COBBLE STITCH

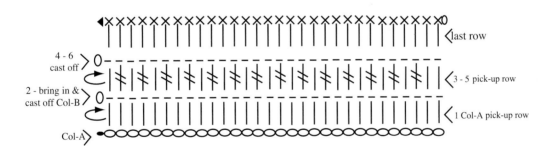

Double treble loop/dtr lp (US treble loop/tr lp)

YO twice, insert hook under st indicated, YO and draw up a loop, YO and draw through one loop, (YO and draw through 2 loops) twice

Foundation row: with col-A make 30 ch.

Row 1: cont. with Col-A draw up a loop in 2nd ch from hook and in each ch across, drop Col-A, turn, slide loops to opp end of hook — 30 lps.

Row 2: with Col-B make slip knot onto hook and cast off as for basic crochenit Row 2 until one loop remains; do not turn.

Row 3: cont. with Col-B draw up a loop in next vertical bar, *dtr lp (US tr lp) under next vertical bar, draw up a loop in next vertical bar, repeat from * across, drop Col-B, turn, slide loops to opp end of hook.

Row 4: pick up Col-A from row below and cast off until one loop remains; do not turn.

Row 5: cont. with Col-A draw up a loop in next vertical bar, *dtr lp (US tr lp) under next vertical bar, draw up a loop in next vertical bar, repeat from * across, drop Col-B, turn, slide loops to opp end of hook.

Row 6: pick up Col-B from row below and cast off until one loop remains; do not turn.

Row 7: cont. with Col-B repeat Row 3.

Repeat Rows 4 to 7 to desired size, ending with Row 4 and finishing with a last row of dc (US sc) under each vertical bar across; finish off.

SQUARE 27: CIRCLET STITCH

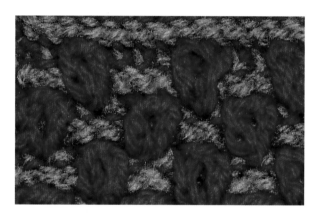

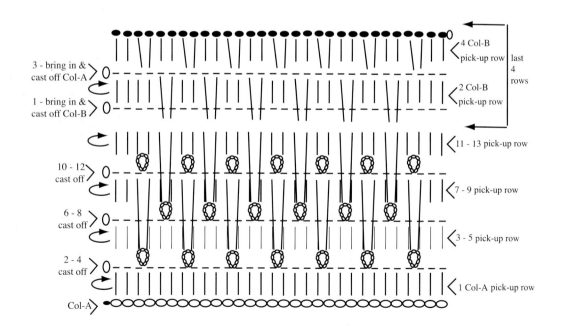

use back bar of chain
skip

circlet st detail

Circlet stitch/circlet st

insert hook into back bar of 4th ch of 9ch loop 4 rows below *and* under next vertical bar, YO and draw up a loop through both (ch bar and vertical bar) at the same time, skip next ch of 9ch loop, insert hook into back bar of next ch of same 9ch loop and under next vertical bar and draw up a loop through both (vertical bar and ch bar) at the same time.

Note: A degree of patience will be required for this pattern until you have become proficient at working the circlet stitch.

Foundation row: with col-A make 30 ch.

Row 1: cont. with Col-A draw up a loop in 2nd ch from hook and in each ch across, drop Col-A, turn, slide loops to opp end of hook — 30 lps.

Row 2: with Col-B make slip knot onto hook and cast off next 2 loops (3 vertical bars made), *9 ch, cast off next 4 loops, repeat from * across to last 3 loops, cast off last 3 loops, do not turn — 7 x 9ch lps.

Row 3: cont. with Col-B and working behind 9ch loops, draw up a loop in each vertical bar across, drop Col-B, turn, slide loops to opp end of hook.

Row 4: pick up Col-A from row below and repeat Row 2; do not turn.

Row 5: cont. with Col-A repeat Row 3, drop Col-A, turn, slide loops to opp end of hook.

Row 6: pick up Col-B from row below and cast off next 5 loops, *9 ch, cast off next 4 loops, repeat from * across to last 5 loops, cast off last 5 loops, do not turn — 6 x 9ch lps.

Row 7: cont. with Col-B draw up a loop under next vertical bar (2 loops on hook), *work circlet st, (working behind 9ch loop of previous row) draw up a loop under next 2 vertical bars and repeat from * across, drop Col-B, turn, slide loops to opp end of hook.

Row 8: pick up Col-A from row below and repeat Row 6.

Row 9: cont. with Col-A repeat Row 7.

Row 10: pick up Col-B from row below and cast off 3 loops, *9 ch, cast off next 4 loops, repeat from * across to last 3 loops, cast off last 3 loops, do not turn — 7 x 9ch lps.

Row 11: cont. with Col-B and working behind 9ch loops, draw up a loop in next 3 vertical bars (4 loops on hook), *work circlet st, draw up a loop under next 2 vertical bars and repeat from * across to last 4 vertical bars, draw up a loop in last 4 vertical bars, drop Col-B, turn, slide loops to opp end of hook.

Row 12: pick up Col-A from row below and repeat Row 10.

Row 13: cont. with Col-A repeat Row 11.

Repeat Rows 6 to 13, stopping 4 rows before last intended row and ending on any Col-B cast-off row.

Next Row: pick up Col-B from row below and cast off as for basic crochenit Row 2; do not turn.

Next Row: cont. with Col-B draw up loops and work circlet st as required, drop Col-B, turn, slide loops to opp end of hook.

Next Row: pick up Col-A and cast off as for basic; do not turn.

Last Row: cont. with Col-A draw up loops and work circlet st as required, but finishing off each stitch with ss.

SQUARE 28: CROCHENIT SLANT STITCH

 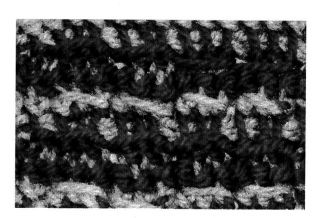

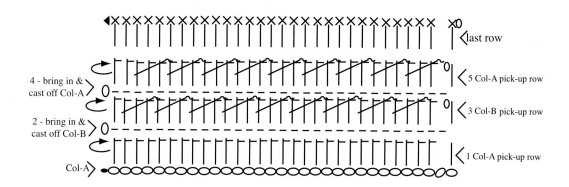

Double crochet loop/dc lp (US single crochet loop/sc lp)

insert hook in next ch or st and draw up a loop, YO and draw through one loop on hook

Slant stitch/slant st: YO (YO loop), dc lp (US sc lp) under next 3 vertical bars, pick up (manually) YO loop and take it off hook across last 3 dc lp (US sc lp) just made

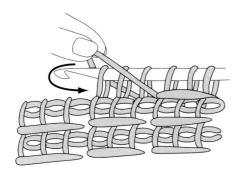

Note: there are **31** ch in the foundation row for this square.

Foundation row: with col-A make 31 ch.

Row 1: cont. with Col-A draw up a loop in 3rd ch from hook and work dc lp (US sc lp) in each ch across, drop Col-A, turn, slide loops to opp end of hook — 30 lps.

Row 2: with Col-B make slip knot onto hook and cast off as for basic crochenit Row 2 until one loop remains; do not turn.

Row 3: cont. with Col-B make 1 ch, dc lp (US sc lp) under next vertical bar, work slant st across to last vertical bar, dc lp (US sc lp) under last vertical bar, drop Col-B, turn, slide loops to opp end of hook

Row 4: pick up Col-A from row below and cast off until one loop remains; do not turn.

Row 5: cont. with Col-A make 1 ch, work slant st across to last 2 vertical bars, dc lp (US sc lp) under last 2 vertical bars, drop Col-A, turn, slide loops to opp end of hook.

Row 6: pick up Col-B from row below and cast off until one loop remains; do not turn.

Row 7: cont. with Col-B repeat Row 3.

Repeat Rows 4 to 7 to desired size, ending with Row 4 and finishing with a last row of dc (US sc) under each vertical bar across; finish off.

SQUARE 29: TWISTED CABLE

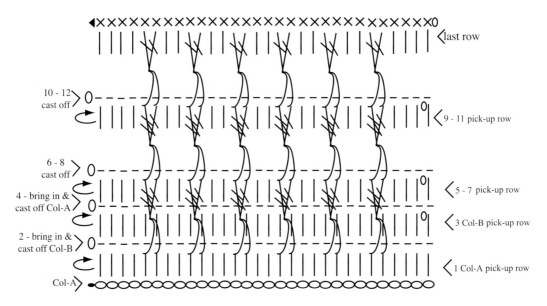

Front Post double treble/FPdtr (US Front Post treble/FPtr)

YO twice, insert hook from front to back around st indicated, YO and draw up a loop, YO and draw through one loop, (YO and draw through 2 loops) twice

Twisted cable stitch/twisted cable st

skip next st, work FPdtr (US FPtr) around next st, work FPdtr (US FPtr) around skipped st

Front Post treble/FPtr (US Front Post double crochet/FPdc)

YO, insert hook from front to back around st indicated, YO and draw up a loop, YO and draw through one loop, YO and draw through 2 loops, YO and draw through 3 loops

Last row twisted cable stitch

skip next st, work FPtr (US FPdc) around next st, work FPtr (FPdc) around skipped st

Foundation row: with col-A make 30 ch.

Row 1: cont. with Col-A draw up a loop in 2nd ch from hook and in each ch across, drop Col-A, turn, slide loops to opp end of hook — 30 lps.

Row 2: with Col-B make slip knot onto hook and cast off as for basic crochenit Row 2 until one loop remains; do not turn.

Row 3: cont. with Col-B make 1 ch, draw up a loop in each vertical bar across, drop Col-B, turn, slide loops to opp end of hook.

Row 4: pick up Col-A from row below and cast off until one loop remains; do not turn.

Row 5: cont. with Col-A make 1 ch, draw up a loop under next 3 vertical bars (4 loops on hook), *work twisted cable st around both loops of next 2 vertical bars directly 4 rows below, draw up a loop under next 2 vertical bars, repeat from * across to last 4 vertical bars, draw up a loop in last 4 vertical bars, drop Col-A, turn, slide loops to opp end of hook.

Row 6: pick up Col-B from row below and cast off until one loop remains; do not turn.

Row 7: cont. with Col-B repeat Row 5.

Row 8: pick up Col-A from row below and cast off until one loop remains; do not turn.

Row 9: cont. with Col-A make 1 ch, draw up a loop under next 3 vertical bars (4 loops on hook), * work twisted cable st around FPdtr directly 4 rows below, draw up a loop under next 2 vertical bars, repeat from * across, to last 4 vertical bars, draw up a loop in last 4 vertical bars, drop Col-A, turn, slide loops to opp end of hook.

Row 10: pick up Col-B from row below and cast off until one loop remains; do not turn.

Row 11: cont. with Col-B repeat Row 9.

Repeat Rows 8 to 11 to desired size, ending with Row 8 and finishing with a last row of dc (US sc) under each vertical bar and last row twisted cable st where required across; finish off.

SQUARE 30: CROCHENIT POPCORN KNIT CHECK

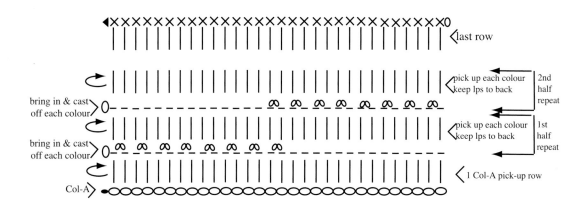

Refer to pattern diagram below for easy stitch placement.

FIRST HALF

Foundation row: with col-A make 30 ch.

Row 1: cont. with Col-A draw up a loop in 2nd ch from hook and in each ch across, drop Col-A, turn, slide loops to opp end of hook — 30 lps.

Row 2: with Col-B make slip knot onto hook and draw through first loop, *2 ch, (YO, draw through 2 loops on hook) twice, repeat from * across to last 15 loops, cast off last 15 loops, do not turn — 8 x 2ch lps.

Row 3: cont. with Col-B and keeping 2ch loop to back of work, draw up a loop in each vertical bar across, drop Col-B, turn, slide loops to opp end of hook.

Row 4: pick up Col-A from row below and draw through one loop, *2 ch, (YO, draw through 2 loops on hook) twice, repeat from * across to last 15 loops, cast off last 15 loops, do not turn — 8 x 2ch lps.

Row 5: cont. with Col-A and keeping 2ch loop to back of work, draw up a loop in each vertical bar across, drop Col-A, turn, slide loops to opp end of hook.

Row 6: pick up Col-B from row below and draw through one loop, *2 ch, (YO, draw through 2 loops on hook) twice, repeat from * across to last 15 loops, cast off last 15 loops, do not turn — 8 x 2ch lps.

Row 7: cont. with Col-B repeat Row 3, drop Col-B, turn, slide loops to opp end of hook.

Repeat Rows 4 to 7 until half-square is completed, finishing on Row 5 (30 Col-A loops on hook).

SECOND HALF
(reverse order)

Row 8: pick up Col-B from row below and cast off first 15 loops, *2 ch, (YO, draw through 2 loops on hook) twice, repeat from * across to last loop, cast off last loop; do not turn.

Row 9: cont. with Col-B and keeping 2ch loop to back of work, draw up a loop in each vertical bar across, drop Col-A, turn, slide loops to opp end of hook.

Row 10: pick up Col-A from row below and cast off first 15 loops, *2 ch, (YO, draw through 2 loops on hook) twice, repeat from * across to last loop, cast off last loop; do not turn.

Row 11: cont. with Col-A and keeping 2ch loop to back of work, draw up a loop in each vertical bar across, drop Col-A, turn, slide loops to opp end of hook.

Repeat Rows 8 to 11 to complete square, ending with Row 10 and finishing with a last row of dc (US sc) under each vertical bar across; finish off.

JOINING THE SQUARES

Join the previously worked edgings of the squares using the ordinary crochet hook. Lay out squares according to placement chart or as desired. Pin the squares together, for easier handling working with 2 rows of squares at a time. Take care to always join from the same end for each row being joined.

Now that you have finished all the squares and have them laid out according to the placement chart (or as you prefer), think of your rug as two rugs, side A (Col-A) as one, and side B as the other. Using the front loops only on side A, join all the squares following the instructions, then do the same for side B. The all-round border will bring the rug together and you will have an entirely reversible rug.

13	23	20	9	30
5	27	28	29	12
15	6	26	11	4
7	24	21	18	10
25	3	17	2	16
22	19	8	14	1

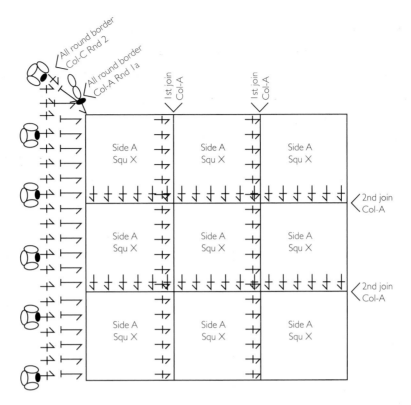

Side A: with side A facing and working from right to left, use front loops only of the squares (outside loops), leaving the back loops (inside loops) unused, and with Col-A join with dc (US sc) in first loops, then dc (US sc) the corresponding loops together to end, finish off.

Repeat this method for 2nd join, working 1 ch when crossing over first join where squares meet.

Side B: with side B facing and working in the unused loops, with Col-B join with dc (US sc) in first loops, then dc (US sc) each corresponding loop together to end; finish off.

Repeat this method for 2nd join, working 1 ch when crossing over first join where squares meet.

ALL-ROUND BORDER

Round 1a: when all squares are joined, with side A facing and working in front loops only, join Col-A with ss in front loop of any corner st, 2 ch, 2 htr (US hdc) in same st, *htr (US hdc) in each st across to next corner st, 3 htr (US hdc) in corner st, repeat from * around, join with ss to 2nd ch of beginning ch; finish off.

Round 1b: with side B facing and working in front (unworked) loops, join Col-B with ss in front loop of any corner st, 2 ch, 2 htr (US hdc) in same st, *htr (US hdc) in each st across to next corner st, 3 htr (US hdc) in corner st, repeat from * around, join with ss to 2nd ch of beginning ch; finish off.

Round 2: with side A facing and working in back loops of Round 1a and 1b (centre loops), join Col-C with dc (US sc) in any corner st, (picot st, dc [US sc]) in same st, *dc (US sc) in next 4 sts, picot st, across to next corner st, (dc [US sc], picot st, dc [US sc]) in corner sts, repeat from * around, join with ss to first dc (US sc); finish off.

Picot stitch: make 1 dc (US sc) in next st, 3 ch, then ss in 3rd ch from hook (picot made).

SUPPLIERS

YARNS

AUSTRALIA

The yarns used for the projects in this book are by Panda and Patons, along with a generic from Lincraft, and can be purchased (or substituted with other 8-ply yarns) from major retailers across Australia such as Spotlight, Lincraft, Kmart and Big W, and from most craft shops that stock wool and other yarns.

Bendigo Woollen Mills
Lansell Street
Bendigo VIC 3550
Ph. (03) 5442 4600
Fax (03) 5442 2918

USA

Bendigo Woollen Mills
Ph. 1 888 235 1993 (1–5 pm, Sunday through Thursday)

Wordwide yarn suppliers list:
www.textilelinks.com/yarn.html

HOOKS

AUSTRALIA

Standard hooks are readily available from major retailers across Australia, such as Spotlight, Lincraft, Kmart and Big W, and from most craft shops.

Tunisian hooks are available from Spotlight and selected craft shops.

Double-ended (crochenit or cro) *hooks* are available from
Crochet Australia
PO Box 126
Wamuran Qld 4512
www.crochetaustralia.com.au
Ph./fax (07) 5496 6826

Crochet Australia supplies all crochet needs except yarn, and delivers worldwide.

USA AND UK
www.wrights.com

www.craft-fair.co.uk